Collective Education in the Kibbutz

from infancy to maturity

edited by

A.I. RABIN &
BERTHA HAZAN

SP

SPRINGER PUBLISHING COMPANY, INC.

Copyright © 1973

SPRINGER PUBLISHING COMPANY, INC.
200 Park Avenue South, New York, N.Y. 10003

Library of Congress Catalog Number: 73-80602
ISBN Number: 0-8261-1470-9

Acknowledgments We would like to thank the following people for allowing us to use their photographs in the book. Listed in order of appearance: Moshe Lapidot, Kibbutz Mizra; Dov Amitai, Kibbutz Gal-On; Hannia Nahor, Kibbutz Lehavot Habashan; Gideon Ras, Kibbutz Revadim; I. Dranger, Kibbutz Sarid; Dov Amitai, Kibbutz Gal-On; Asher Ben-Arie, Kibbutz Hazorea; Riva Segal, Kibbutz Barkai; Dov Amitai, Kibbutz Gal-On; I. Dranger, Kibbutz Sarid.

Printed in U.S.A.

CONTENTS

INTRODUCTION
Bertha Hazan   1

EARLY CHILDHOOD EDUCATION
Frieda Katz and Gideon Lewin   11

*The family: parent-child relations 11 — The extended family 14
— The parental role in habit training 15 — The babies' and
toddlers' house 16 — The babies' home 17 — The toddlers'
house 21 — Persons who influence the child's development 24 —
Identification and identity 25 — The positive value of two
persons as objects of identification 26 — Education of the
"ego" 29*

THE KINDERGARTEN
Miriam Roth   35

*The parents' home 37 — Celebration of holidays 38 — Activities
in the kindergarten ´39 — The kindergarten staff 41 — Emotional
problems 42 — First grade (the "interim" year) 44 — The kibbutz
society 46*

THE JUNIOR CHILDREN'S COMMUNITY
Hava Shamir   49

*Socialization and individualization 50 — The attitude toward the
adult world of parents and kibbutz members 51 — How the
junior children's society functions 52*

THE PROJECT METHOD: ELEMENTARY SCHOOLS
Lea Alterman   63

*Principles of the project method 64 — The annual program of
projects 72 — The integration of subjects 78 — Language
teaching in the project method 82 — The teaching of mathematics in the project method 83 — Teaching outside the framework of the project method 85 — The group and the teacher-
counselor 88 — The desire for achievement rather than competition for grades 90 — The means and goals of education 93 —
Conclusion 93*

268786

THE YOUTH SOCIETY
Moni Alon   97

Changes in the educational group during adolescence 100 — The role of teacher-counselors 103 — Coeducation and sex education 105 — Ideological education 110 — Education for work 117 — Relationships with parents during adolescence 120 — Relationships with the kibbutz, the adult society, and self-realization 123 — Stability and change 126

METHODS OF STUDY AND INSTRUCTION IN HIGH SCHOOL
Zvi Lavi   131

Theoretical origins of the project method 134 — Experimental schools which influence us 135 — Principal modifications of the project method 137 — Principles of learning in the secondary school (ages 12-18) 139 — Social principles. Nonselective education 139 — Unity of education and instruction 143 — The peer-group unit 144 — Education for work 145 — Cooperation between teachers and students. Directed independence 146 — Psychological-educational principles 147 — Didactic principles of the project method 156

SPECIAL EDUCATION AND CHILD GUIDANCE CLINIC   161
Rachel Manor

ORANIM–PEDAGOGICAL CENTER OF THE KIBBUTZIM
Menahem Gerson   171

The structure of Oranim. Its advantages 172 — Pedagogical principles 173 — What we emphasize 174 — Problems awaiting solution 175 — Two important courses 176 — The institute of research on kibbutz education 178

EPILOGUE
A.I. Rabin   181

References   183

Glossary   184

CONTRIBUTORS

Moni Alon. Lecturer in sociology, Oranim; formerly Director, Educational Department, Kibbutz Artzi.

Lea Alterman. Teacher, Supervisor of Elementary Schools, Kibbutz Artzi; editor (deceased).

Menahem Gerson, Ph.D. Research Director, Oranim Center for the Study of Kibbutz Education.

Bertha Hazan. Editor. *Sifriat Poalim* (an educational publication), Tel Aviv.

Frieda Katz. Supervisor, Department of Early Childhood Education, Kibbutz Artzi.

Zvi Lavi. Director, Educational Department, Kibbutz Artzi.

Gideon Lewin. Lecturer on child psychology, Kibbutz Teacher Training School, Oranim.

Rachel Manor. Director, Oranim Child Guidance Clinic.

A.I. Rabin, Ph.D. Professor of Psychology, Michigan State University.

Miriam Roth, M.A. Teacher of Pedagogics, Oranim.

Hava Shamir. Teacher; Supervisor of Elementary Schools, Kibbutz Artzi.

PREFACE

Much has been written about kibbutz child-rearing and education. Most accounts of this innovative and interesting system in the communal setting have been written by outsiders—"looking in," so to speak—mainly American social scientists: psychologists, anthropologists, psychiatrists, and others.

Many of these descriptions have been rather brief and have often been included in the context of broader ethnographic or descriptive studies of kibbutz society as a whole. Other accounts have appeared in conjunction with research reports, of varying degrees of rigor, which have attempted to scrutinize the effects of kibbutz child-rearing. To date there has been no detailed and comprehensive statement of the kibbutz educational approach and experience by those who have been primarily involved in it. It might be said, therefore, that the present volume represents a "look from within"—a statement by kibbutz educators themselves.

Ten veteran educators of the kibbutz movement have combined their efforts in presenting this detailed story of various aspects and phases of kibbutz education. Some of the contributors have been associated with this educational effort from its very inception, having witnessed and participated in the gradual evolution of the kibbutz child-rearing and educational process—from infancy to maturity. They have been involved in the development of methods to prepare and create the "new man," the new kibbutz generation that will be ready to take over from those who were brought up in the conventional family setting and in the traditional educational system.

In the introductory chapter, Bertha Hazan, who has been a leading force in kibbutz education for well over a generation, presents the broad historical and philosophical perspectives of that movement. Frieda Katz and Gideon Levin, active educators, researchers, and child psychologists, describe (in Chapter 2) the first four years in the life of the kibbutz child. Both have had considerable experience in working directly with children as well as in training teachers and metaplot (child-care workers) for the kibbutz children's houses. Chapter 3 was authored by Miriam Roth, a veteran kindergarten teacher and trainer of teachers, with broad experience in Israel and abroad.

Chapters 4 and 5 deal with two important aspects of the pre-adolescent experience in the kibbutz. Hava Shamir describes a fascinating and viable experiment: "the children's society," a sort of junior, semiautonomous kibbutz that is so important in the development of the unique kibbutz character and personality. A parallel statement of the more formal educational and learning procedures of this age group is presented by Lea Alterman. Here the "project method " and progressive education in its successful reincarnation, are highlighted.

A similar pair of chapters covers the adolescent period. In Chapter 6, Moni Alon, an experienced high school teacher and sociologist, discusses the society of adolescents in the kibbutz: its ideological training, the question of sex relations, and the preparation of the adolescent peer society for the adult world.

This description is followed by the contribution, in Chapter 7, of the long-time educator and author, Zvi Lavi, who outlines the theoretical and psychological origins of the educational system and illustrates the substantive aspects of the study program.

In the final chapters, two special and unique programs of the overall educational undertaking are considered. Rachel Manor (Chapter 8) clearly shows that kibbutz children are not "problem-free." She describes a unique special-education project in which a large network of workers is guided by a central professional corps in their day-to-day activities with youngsters who require special help for a wide range of emotional and educational problems. In Chapter 9 Dr. Menahem Gerson, one of the guiding spirits of the kibbutz college of education, offers an interesting analysis of the rationale for a special teacher training institute. Within the structure of the unique kibbutz society, Gerson points out, a somewhat unconventional training program is required for teachers in the innovative schools.

The overall impression is that this educational enterprise is not one of an exotic or primitive society which anthropologists and general readers may find "interesting." On the contrary, the reader becomes aware of the conscious effort of a modern society, with a Western orientation, to provide continuity to the social structure it has erected. In these days, when America is casting about for alternative models and solutions in the field of child-rearing and education, there is much that can be gained from the rich experience related in this volume. The modifications in the family structure, and their relationship to the socioeducational matrix of kibbutz society, give the reports presented here a considerable relevance and timeliness.

A.I. Rabin
East Lansing, Michigan

ACKNOWLEDGMENT

The assistance of Mr. Dennis Fox in the editing of the manuscript and of Rita Bernier in its preparation is hereby gratefully acknowledged.

vii

collective education encompasses the totality of the child's life

Introduction

by Bertha Hazan

The kibbutz movement is not a utopian movement. Its members do not seek to better their lot by escaping the life around them, nor do they wish to isolate themselves within idyllic rural communes. True, the kibbutz as a pattern of life represents a goal in itself. We want this life, in which we are granted the opportunity to build with our own hands the cells of a new cooperative society, in which there are neither exploiters nor exploited; a society in which each works according to his ability and receives from the community according to his needs, and where the only limitation is the economic capacity of the society to produce and render services. However, we know that this life of ours will continue to flourish only if it constitutes an inseparable part of the new national and societal life taking shape in our country. For us, therefore, the kibbutz is also a means in our struggle for the continued building and coalescence of our national life as a progressive society whose goal is a socialist society.

As an ideological and politically militant movement, the kibbutz must take part in the sociopolitical struggles of our country. On the one hand, in order to influence the forces outside of the kibbutz, the kibbutz movement is alert and sensitive to all national events and developments. On the other hand, our movement not only influences the life of the country, but is in turn influenced by external factors. The kibbutz must resist any influences that are alien to its social-ideological tenets and infiltrate it in various ways. In defending its life-pattern against negative phenomena, the main weapon of the kibbutz is its social strength, its cultural crystallization, and its political-ideological consolidation. The most important means of crystallizing kibbutz life and assuring its continuity is education, which occupies a central position among the concerns of all currents within the kibbutz.

The first kibbutz—Deganya—was established in Palestine in 1909, with only 12 members. Today, the kibbutz movement numbers 226 kibbutzim, with a population of about 90,000, including 31,400 children and youth. It is organized into three large federations and one small federation (which serves a religious movement). Each federation differs in political outlook, but the social goals of all are fundamentally identical. They also vary in their respective structures and in the practical realization of their goals. Consequently, it is natural for these differences to find expression in the educational sphere.

TABLE 1

Children and Youth in the Kibbutzim (1970)

	Children born in the kibbutz	Children from outside the kibbutz	Youth groups	Total
Kibbutz Artzi	9,485	568	749	10,802
Ichud	8,688	704	706	10,098
Kibbutz Meuchad	7,204	900	780	8,884
Kibbutz Dati	1,447	106	76	1,629
(a religious movement)				
	26,824	2,278	2,311	31,413

Their fundamentally identical social goals constitute the bases for the joint organization of all kibbutz movements in the Union of Kibbutz Movements (Brit Hatnua Hakibbutzit). The Union maintains a series of joint institutions and enterprises that do not impinge upon the autonomy of any of its affiliates. At the center of these joint enterprises is the Oranim Teacher Training College, where the house-mothers (metaplot), kindergarten teachers, and elementary and high school teachers of the three large federations acquire their professional training. The three kibbutz federations are Kibbutz Artzi Hashomer Hatzair, Ichud Hakibbutzim Ve'hakvutzot, and Kibbutz Meuchad.

The kibbutz movement began as one of age-peers—its founders were all young people. Today, the grandchildren of the founders are beginning to integrate into the life of the movement, and the structural center of gravity is shifting from the first to the second generation. With the passage of years, the kibbutz has changed from a young and ethically motivated, albeit simplistic, commune to a communal society with a wealth of assets and powerful means of production as well as rich and complex sociocultural patterns. The needs of its members have become more diversified, and its public services have expanded and improved. This is a society to which nothing human—sorrows or joys—is alien. Increasingly, it links the deep-rootedness of rural life and a high level of cultural and spiritual awareness.

The kibbutz movement also began as a cooperative agricultural movement. It has always considered the upbuilding of a communal economy as the central task of our national rebirth. However, after the establishment of the State of Israel and its rapid industrial development, the entire kibbutz movement began to integrate industry into its agriculture. Today, the kibbutz is becoming a communal agroindustrial entity. The social and organizational development of the kibbutz, and the merging of agriculture and industry, place new demands on the kibbutz in the areas of education and learning. As a result, the level of expertise in coping with these problems has risen.

Cultural and scientific-technological progress has transformed the kibbutz into a rural community that is among the most economically advanced in the world. The merging of agriculture and industry requires a higher sociocultural level and an even higher scientific-technological capacity for the continued building of a communal society. And it is this very merger which also engenders new possibilities for expanding and deepening our educational undertaking, the *sine qua non* for ongoing social, cultural, and economic development. Our education and learning must reach out—and it is beginning to do so—beyond the limits of the instructional framework of training which hitherto terminated at the age of 18.

However, as opposed to a trend that is becoming increasingly prominent in our country and abroad—a trend that is deepening the rift between the natural sciences and technology, on the one hand, and the social and cultural life of man on the other—we aspire to fuse every area of human creativity and to place technology at the service of people instead of making the technologist the ruler and subjugator of society. To that end, we strive to effect a harmonious fusion between cultural creativity and physical endeavor, and to do away with such a contradiction in present-day society. We are certain that the linking of agriculture and industry within the framework of the kibbutz will enhance this aspiration, without which a new society is inconceivable. And it is this aspiration which guides our instructional and educational work.

Collective education is a product of kibbutz society, which bases every aspect of its life on mutual aid and unlimited reciprocal responsibility, as well as on equality and sharing. Collective education has grown organically out of this social milieu. The relationship between the educational system and the social essence of the kibbutz and its aspirations has endowed collective education with its form and content. Kibbutz society has given rise to an educational framework that is appropriate to its sociocollective essence and reflects its way of life, its cultural and moral values. Indeed, the interpenetration of all these factors and values is the only guarantee of the effectiveness of our educational system and of its ability to fulfill its goals. All of collective education—its methods and means, the relationship between the learning process and education, the organizational structure and social content—embodies the basic sociocultural, moral, and ideational values of the kibbutz movement.

However, it is not merely a societal point of departure that has guided us in crystallizing the framework and essence of our educational work. We have also learned much from the European movements of the 1920s, when a critique of schools and traditional education was initiated. We were influenced by the free-thinking youth movements of Europe and, in particular, by the pioneer youth movement Hashomer Hatzair, whose senior members founded the Hashomer Hatzair kibbutzim in Israel. We were helped greatly by the achievements of innovators who centered their educational work on the emotional needs of the child and on giving due consideration to his abilities and specific spiritual character. In all these searchings our directive principle was the desire to educate a self-contained personality, which, conscious of its inner freedom, would coalesce with society and with societal aspirations and struggles. We have never ignored the fact that man as an individual, and society as a whole, constitute a unity characterized by both constant struggle and constant identification. Our goal has been the achievement of social completeness, not through the deprivation of individual development but, rather, through each person's maximal development.

We have opened our educational establishment to the influence of all these factors, aware of and ready to learn from every progressive experiment by others. However, even though such influences have exerted a considerable impact on collective education, we have not mechanically introduced any form of education which took shape under conditions that differed from ours. We *did* attempt to adapt them to our specific reality. From its very inception, the image of collective education was shaped by discussions that involved both educators and the entire kibbutz community. Our system of education, transcending the family framework, becomes an asset of the social group as a whole, and can be structured only by the endeavors of the total group. It must be guided by clearly defined socioeducational objectives that are achieved by group consensus. The unique conditions of the kibbutz permit the practical application of theoretical concepts. The concern for teaching and educating the younger generation has become an inseparable part of the life of each kibbutz and of the overall kibbutz movement.

Thus, organically, and thanks to a powerful and creative thrust, we have developed a uniform and uninterrupted system of collective education—from the infants' home to the education of adolescents.

In the upbringing of our children, collective education fulfills most consistently the *element of equality*. This is not a mechanically applied external equality, but a value-equality, ensuring *each child*, without exception, the possibility of exploiting every latent ability and talent. This principle is applied from birth through adulthood. It not only guides us in crystallizing our pedagogical awareness, but is a vital adjunct of the equality that essentially determines our communal way of life. Kibbutz society, which assumes the full responsibility for the education and destiny of all its children, has consummated this vital imperative in actual practice.

The kibbutz represents an attempt to effect an all-encompassing social revolution. Instead of a society based on antagonisms and premised on the splintering and atomization of all spheres of life, we have set up the cells of an integral society. This realignment of life-patterns has, of necessity, engendered a fundamental realignment in the field of education. The center of gravity of educational practice has passed from the exclusive control by the family to the social group. Some responsibilities which hitherto rested mainly with parents—for example, behavioral habit training and impulse control—are now being handled by teacher-educators on behalf of the entire kibbutz community. As a result, collective education encompasses the totality of the child's life: care of the body and health, learning and upbringing, work and social life.

Despite the priority of societal factors, collective education has not been impervious to the *decisive educational value* of the unique emotional link between parent and child. We have never doubted the importance of this relationship for the normal development of children. Well-functioning emotional ties in the family constitute one of the most vital elements in securing the healthy development of the younger generation. And we are ever mindful that the success of our educational process is largely determined by the interaction of the parental home and the children's home.

Indeed, this interaction has worked—it has met the test of reality. The relations between parents and children have not been impaired by collective education; in fact, they have actually become more profound. The daily tensions so prevalent in child-parent relationships no longer becloud the home. Except for deviant cases, family relations of affection and deep friendship are formed when the child is very young. The foundations are laid for the development of firm, harmonious ties during adolescence, ties that become solidified in the friendship of lifetime partners.

One of the chief fundamentals of collective education is the *unity of the determining educational factors:* parents, the adult society in the kibbutz, the teacher-counsellors, and the children's society. In contrast with education outside kibbutz society, which is generally characterized by constant contradiction and tension between the basic educational factors, the unity in the kibbutz system stems from the very nature of kibbutz life. To achieve maximum utilization of all the potentialities of this unity, the educational workers in each educational unit must function on the basis of conscious cooperation—first and foremost, between educators and parents, as well as between educators and the kibbutz as a whole. Such cooperation is the prime prerequisite for our entire educational enterprise. And, we repeat, the objective conditions for this unity are inherent in kibbutz society.

Collective education is premised upon modern psychology and, in particular, on psychoanalysis, which has researched deeply into the laws of the development of the child and the adolescent and has elaborated the needs, abilities, and tendencies of each age level as a basis for fruitful educational work. We adhere faithfully to the premise that the child and his life constitute a goal in themselves, that only to the extent that we enable him to live out the stages of his development to his maximal emotional and spiritual capacity will his crystallization as an adult—at peace with himself, creatively integrated within society—be achieved.

This psychological-pedagogical approach has been developed in an unceasing effort to adapt it to the realities of kibbutz life. It has become the guiding principle of all our educational work, a principle on the basis of which we continue to consolidate our educational theory.

We have devoted special attention to establishing the *scientific-psychological premises for our work with prekindergarten youngsters.* This is the age when dominant moods, habits, and emotional trends are determined, with the help of which it is possible, at later ages, to strengthen the individual's conscious control over his drives and to direct these drives into positive, constructive, and creative channels. We place special emphasis on education at this age and on its practical application through close cooperation with parents—especially with the mother. The results are palpable as education continues in the more advanced age groups.

Our entire educational program is based on *social education.* The desire to stress *loyalty to the community*, combined with ensuring the *individual* development of each child, led us, at the very beginning, to set up the *educational group* and the *children's society* as our chief instruments.

The importance of the *educational group* is that it creates a framework, a way of life most suited to the needs of any given age level. This relatively limited framework, embracing every aspect of the young child's life—studies and work, play and discussion, trips and life together in a shared home—envelops him in a democratic, intimate, and straightforward atmosphere, and is the basis of relations of friendship and companionship among members of the group. Guided by the counselor-teacher, the group serves as the instrument for educating the individual. In it, the incipient crystallization of social and human values is assured, as is social morality, without which kibbutz life could not exist.

The *children's society*, on the other hand, forms the broader framework for the desired balance between the education of the individual, the enhancement of personal attributes and individual abilities, and education for communal life. This framework provides wide scope for the creative activity of each person, while at the same time deepening a sense of responsibility toward the society which he is already building at an early age.

However, the most decisive stage in the crystallization of social education is the high school (mosad chinuchi). This framework for living, as we understand it, is in consonance with the adolescent and with his psychological makeup. Here the adolescent experiences a richly endowed life of work, study, and social activity. He is responsible for what takes place in his social sphere, and he actively struggles for the formation and maintenance of its social values. And this is done in the course of cooperation with the counsellor-educators—a process that gives *genuine experience in communal living*. The young people's society simultaneously serves as the local cell of the youth movement, which eventually becomes part of the Hashomer Hatzair youth movement.

We have travelled a very long road since our first experiment in collective education more than forty years ago. We have learned much during those years, and have changed and perfected many things. Developments within the overall kibbutz movement have been reflected (and will continue to be reflected) in our educational system—the process is still far from complete. Nevertheless, it is a fact that at the present time, when the weight of basic social, intellectual, and moral values within society has been declining, our collective education has succeeded in bequeathing to our children the urge for a way of life in which moral and social values predominate. Delinquency and sexual deviations are almost nonexistent among our children. And thousands of children reared in our collective system of education have become part and parcel of the social and economic creativity of the kibbutz and are increasingly becoming the decisive factor within it. Only a small minority of kibbutz "products" abandon it.

We do have problems, some of which have not been resolved. Our main difficulties are connected with the implementation of our program. Our favorable experiences substantiate the validity of our theory and principles of collective education, which undoubtedly represents one of the most significant innovations of the kibbutz movement. We believe, too, that it can also offer some insight into the complex educational problems confronting educators throughout the world.

This collection of articles is devoted to a description of the educational programs of the 73 kibbutzim of Hashomer Hatzair's Kibbutz Artzi. The participants who prepared this collection have for many years been intimately involved in kibbutz educational work; each writer specializes in a key sector, ranging from infant care to high school education and teacher training. This wide spectrum of specialization presented some disadvantages—for example, we were unable to avoid some repetition when each writer attempted to describe the underlying elements in a particular sector. However, there is a compensating aspect: each chapter constitutes a self-contained unit, which is bound to facilitate matters for a reader who is interested in a particular area of our educational program. In summary, it seems to us, the favorable points outweigh the unfavorable ones.

parents are the key factors in the child's . . . development

Early Childhood Education

by Frieda Katz and Gideon Lewin

The Family: Parent-Child Relations

Kibbutz life patterns are the result of its own experiences and have effected basic changes in all human relationships, including those in the family. Under the conditions of communal life, where the principle of equality between the sexes in every sphere of life obtains, the family has lost its patriarchal stamp.

Objective conditions in the kibbutz necessitated the search for new educational methods, methods that would not conflict with our social framework. The underlying principle of our educational system is the task of the kibbutz to educate and support every child from birth until the assumption of adult responsibility.

Teaching the child to master infantile urges—the habit training so vital to his development—is a function carried out mainly by educators in the children's home. Because these educators are able to maintain objective

11

and professional attitudes, fewer problems are encountered than is generally the case when child-rearing takes place in the conventional family setting and parents have the full-time responsibility.

At first, nonkibbutz observers felt that our parents would lose all contact with their children, and that the central figures in the child's life would by the metapelet and the educators, not the mother and father. But our experience has proved the opposite: parent-child relations are very strong, even though the child spends most of his days and nights in the children's house. The reason may be found in the emotional content of these contacts, for kibbutz education to a large extent reduces the parent-child conflicts that are generally part and parcel of traditional family life. Our system tends to create freer, less tense relations; the image and status of parents in the eyes of their children do not depend on *external authority*—not even the father's, because the kibbutz family retains no patriarchal characteristics. Yet the great wealth of our experience reinforces the view that parents are the key factor in the child's education and healthy development, and that there can be no substitute for them. The parents' home occupies the central place in the emotional life of the small child, instilling in him his primary attitude toward the kibbutz and its society. To a great extent, indeed, the personal human values absorbed in the parents' home mold the young child's personality.

The ideal concept of the traditional upbringing of children envisages round-the-clock contact with the parent as the child gradually and naturally becomes part of the fabric of family life. A mother need not devote any particular effort to discover ways of "having a good time" with a child who is with her all the time. Such an idealized picture, however, fails to take into consideration the difficulties of bringing up children in a home that is not designed specifically to meet the needs of youngsters. It fails to take into account the restrictions which parents, as well as the daily routines of the home, impose upon the child. Conflicts arise because of the different interests and habits of adults and children. In addition, we find that constant proximity and inevitable competition and quarrels between siblings compel parents to intervene, despite the fact that this intervention may not always be consistent with a child's capacity to understand.

The child living with his parents is not, by virtue of this fact, immune to feelings of alienation and loneliness, to errors and failures, or even to the anxiety and fear of being emotionally abandoned. Above all, he is not protected against shocks within the family, such as the lengthy absence of a parent because of illness, divorce, or death. Of course, such situations also affect a kibbutz child, and undoubtedly harm him emotionally, particularly if they occur during his early years. But their effects are not as grave as they tend to be in traditional family life because, in the kibbutz, so many factors in the child's life remain stable despite the calamity: the children's house, the other children, the permanent educational staff, and the established routines—factors that strengthen the child and help him to cope with crises.

The daily schedule in the kibbutz is so arranged that parents can spend time in their own quarters with their children for several hours after work. Here is an example of one such arrangement: The family sits down to afternoon tea, and the parents and children discuss the day's events or some current affairs. The youngest child plays in a corner, and an older brother or sister occasionally joins in.

A significant change in the kibbutz family structure can be gauged by examining the father's status. No longer a patriarchal figure, his educational function now assumes the greatest importance. His authority is not external; rather, it emanates from his personal traits, which are the basis for ties of friendship with his children. He participates actively in all stages of their upbringing, and shares with the mother an involvement in almost all questions of education. From the very start of the child's life, the father, like the mother, is a source of emotional satisfaction. The child sees him engaging in various tasks at work and exercising a role in the community, and is impressed by his overall personality—a factor which later leads to identification with his father and is decisive for the child's normal growth. The father plays and goes for walks with his children, and is looked up to as a close friend. Small boys generally feel a strong attachment to their fathers, sometimes more so than to their mothers.

The child anticipates the daily encounter with his parents not in a "state of tension," as is argued by critics of kibbutz education, but with positive expectations that usually culminate in a feeling of satisfaction. The pleasurable anticipation of such meetings is an organic part of the child's life. In this context, we may note the conclusion drawn by Erik Erikson that restrictions imposed by a society which arise organically from the life of that community do not have a negative effect; rather, they are instrumental in molding a personality that is in harmony with that community.

When the time comes for parents and child to part at bedtime, one or both of the parents bring him to the children's house, undress him or help him undress, and get him ready for bed. They often take this opportunity to discuss with the metapelet the child's daytime activities, to look at his work, or to observe a new arrangement in the house and classroom.

Most youngsters respond with a matter-of-fact "good night" to their parents' farewell; *the leave-taking is rarely problematic*. In some cases, however, a child is reluctant to part with his parents—due to conflicts within the nuclear family or other problems. If that occurs, one or both of the parents will remain until the child falls asleep, and will do so until the problem has been overcome.

We would like to underscore a dynamic quality of kibbutz life: we remain constantly alert to the challenge of new problems. Our second generation of parents tends to differ from their elders with respect to the balance between the two centers of a child's life—the parents' home and the children's house. The newer generation places greater emphasis on the role of the family than did the founders of the kibbutz. Some mothers, for example, prefer to spend more time with their children than the kibbutz can allocate to a working woman. (It should be noted that during the first year of the child's life the mother enjoys a very short workday.) An examination of this tendency is now under way, and its ideological and educational implications, as well as its practical aspects, are being discussed.

The Extended Family

The present kibbutz population is composed of two, three, and in rare instances, four generations living together in a single kibbutz. This has brought changes in the general pattern of kibbutz life, in terms of its socioeconomic and educational features.

For the small child, the "family circle" means not only his parents and siblings, as in the past, but also his grandparents, aunts, uncles, and cousins. His "extended family" gives the child a feeling of greater security. In today's kibbutz, parents and children live in the only known "extended family" in Western society. In other parts of the world, such families are based on the authority of the family head, but the kibbutz extended family is based on nuclear family units that are basically independent of each other. In the absence of any model, we are creating our own patterns.

It should be remembered that, for the kibbutz child, there are two focal points: the family and the parents' home, on the one hand, and the children's group and metapelet on the other. Any upset in the balance between these two centers would hinder normal development, since together they represent the primary world of the kibbutz child's life. Everything else—the home of a grandmother, of an uncle, of a brother or sister—is a *secondary center,* reinforcing the two primary centers with respect to security.

Grandparents in the kibbutz extend the lifeline of the family and deepen its roots. Their life experience enhances their ability to offer. aid and advice to the young family.

The Parental Role in Habit Training

Habit training—teaching the child to eat independently, to maintain cleanliness, to accept schedules, routines, and social discipline—is often a source of conflict, particularly when the child is between two and five years old. During that period, relations between parents and child—which always involve instinctual elements on both sides—become the child's central problem. Even parents who are generally stable may commit errors and be prone to inappropriate emotional reactions. However, when the educational system frees parents from making the chief demands upon the child's habit-training development, as is the case with the kibbutz system, the tendency toward conflict between parents and children is greatly reduced.

Collective education is especially important in cases where the emotional relations between the child and his parents may disturb the development of the child. The mother-child relationship, particularly in early childhood, involves a wide spectrum of emotional nuances that sometimes cause emotional difficulties for the child—for example, an overanxious mother who worries excessively and pampers him, or a negligent mother who pays too little attention to her children and has too little contact with them.

If there are pathological factors in a mother-child relationship, the kibbutz atmosphere serves as a deterrent. An anxious mother who tries to be overprotective can cause far less harm in the kibbutz setting because there are fewer opportunities; the metapelet, who is permanently in charge of the child, supervises his development. Her objectivity can more easily ensure the early discovery of deviant behavior and disturbances, and she can refer the child for immediate treatment.

No effort is spared in helping the child. One of the means employed is parent guidance, which is aimed at altering the behavior of parents vis-à-vis their child. This guidance is given by the metapelet or, in very difficult cases, in consultation with professionals. The routine advice given by the metapelet—if she is experienced and the mother has confidence in her—is of particular importance in diverting mother-child relations into healthier channels. The presence of the metapelet in the children's house during meals and at other times—caring for the child firmly, but with patience and love, and conveying this love in her manner of speaking, in her play with him, in the attention she gives him—tends to counterbalance the conflicts that frequently exist between mother and child.

With the growth of the kibbutz movement and the realization that there are now hundreds of cases of parent-child problems, careful attention must be given to the personal and professional qualifications of the metapelet, particularly for the early childhood group. Every kibbutz now has one person in charge of what is known as "the tender years"; she supervises all the metaplot, guiding and counselling them in each individual case. The kibbutz movements also maintain departments for counselling by correspondence or through direct contact. Metaplot participate in study groups at regular monthly intervals, where current and urgent educational problems are raised. Metaplot receive their training at the central kibbutz Seminar at Oranim. The training at Oranim, from several months to one or two years, is geared to increasing the effectiveness of the metapelet in her important socioeducational role.

We are presently very much concerned with the training of metaplot because a considerable number of experienced metaplot have reached the age of retirement. Regrettably, this process of withdrawal from child-care work has been too rapid, and the majority of today's metaplot are young women.

The Babies' and Toddlers' House: "The Tender Years"

Social education is of great value at every stage of a child's development. However, nonkibbutz observers have not yet accepted the view that group education meets the child's needs.

The basic children's group in the kibbutz—four to six children who remain in the same group from birth until approximately age four, when they enter kindergarten—forms a fixed setting for the children. The age difference between the oldest and youngest child in the group is usually half a year.

One of the positive values of this system is the sense of *belonging*, of being an important part of (and being firmly rooted in) the company of one's peers. In this way the child's sense of belonging, which at first was anchored in his relations with his parents, extends to the group and then to the entire community. In addition, the miniature collective fosters the child's independence, directing it into desirable channels. It strengthens him in his relations with overanxious or domineering parents who, under other circumstances, would restrict his activity. Instead of encountering anxiety and opposition, which could serve as a constant source of conflicts, the child's attempts at independence result in encouragement and guidance within his group and arouse the appreciation of his parents.

However, we should not overlook the fact that from 18 months to three years, the child is highly egocentric, and life in the small group sometimes engenders conflicts between the child's desire to gratify his own needs and the desires of his peers. At this point, the educational role of the metapelet is of key importance: she must understand the developmental stages of children in general, as well as the individual differences of those in her care, so that she can create an atmosphere that satisfies the needs of each child and reduces tension. For many years we have been conducting research into the problem of "the small child in his own age group," and have been able to establish educational guidelines which, while satisfactory, still require study. Practical guidance for the metapelet in charge of very young children is an urgent task.

Susan Isaacs, the prominent psychologist who investigated the social life of small children, points out that one of the child's basic needs is to find "legitimate" objects for the natural aggression essential to his development. In her view, this need is not met in the traditional contemporary family with few children. In it, emotional relations are sometimes charged with conflict, and it is difficult for the child to express aggressiveness towards his parents. He rejects them, and psychological damage may ensue.

This phenomenon is not seen in the kibbutz educational system. In the children's group, the relations among the children (and between them and the metapelet) are such that the child can express his aggressive feelings freely and directly—mainly, it is true, in positive ways, such as games and ample motor activity, but also in outright expressions of rage, jealousy, or crying—without fear of punishment.

The Babies' Home

The kibbutz babies' house is the first setting in the child's life. The typical house has two wings, with four to six infants in each. The child now belongs to a specific group, which has its own metapelet, specially trained in baby care and in all problems connected with mother-infant relations.

When the mother first brings the infant to the babies' house, the metapelet does her best to instill confidence that the house serves baby *and* parents. The crib is decorated with toys, a vase of flowers awaits the mother, and small gifts made by friends or by mothers of other babies in the unit are laid out.

A warm atmosphere prevails: the house is open to the young couple, to the grandparents, or to siblings at all hours of the day. Since the new mother does not have to return to work for six weeks after giving birth, she is free to devote herself to her baby and to rest. The metapelet gives encouragement and aid, for the psychological link between mother and child during the early months and years of life is the basis for the child's future development.

Breast-feeding—apart from its beneficial advantage in terms of health— is undoubtedly one of the most important means of forging this powerful link, and is encouraged. The norms for maternity benefits, established by the kibbutz movement's Education Department and the National Conference of Infant Nurses, ensure the mother every suitable condition during the nursing and weaning period.

Norms for Maternity Benefits

1. An expectant mother whose pregnancy is normal will work full-time, but it is recommended that she remain at the same job, particularly during the last six months of pregnancy.
2. During the last six weeks before the expected date of birth, she works four hours a day or, if she desires, six hours.
3. The mother is free from all work for six weeks after giving birth.
4. When the infant is six weeks old, and until it becomes six months old, the mother works four hours a day. After that, the hours are gradually increased until, when the baby is one year old, she resumes full-time work.
5. The babies' home must provide the mother with the most comfortable conditions possible and allow her to be alone with her child when she is nursing. The practical arrangements for this are always facilitated by the metapelet.
6. In the event of the mother's absense, due to illness or any other unavoidable cause, the metapelet will enlist the aid of the father in caring for the baby.

A mother who does not have breast milk, or who for any other reason is unable to breast-feed her infant, is provided with the same conditions as the nursing mother. She bottle-feeds her baby until he is weaned.

At first the infant is fed five times daily, with the schedule established according to the baby's demands. If the baby cries before its scheduled feeding time, the metapelet can summon the mother by telephone or, if the mother prefers to rest, bottle-feed the infant. A night nurse feeds the infants until they sleep through the night, but a mother who prefers to do this herself is free to nurse her baby at night.

The mothers generally enjoy feeding their babies together in a friendly, relaxed atmosphere. However, if some mothers are unable to nurse their babies in company—one woman may be embarrassed or inhibited, another may prefer to be alone—the schedule is arranged so that the mother can nurse when others are not present, or she uses another room in the babies' home.

After the first six weeks, during which she has been completely free, the mother returns to work—at first for only four hours a day—and continues to breast- or bottle-feed her infant. This period is usually an enriching one for the mother despite her increased duties: she is devoting herself to her baby, sometimes to an older child who is now more demanding, and she also participates in the work routines of the kibbutz.

Weaning takes place gradually, usually at the end of the fifth month, and is completed when the baby is about nine to twelve months old. The slow transition from suckling to drinking from a cup and spoon, and, at a later date, to eating solid foods, helps the infant to adapt to new ways of eating and to prepared foods. If a mother is reluctant to wean her baby, the metapelet assists in overcoming the difficulty.

The weaning process is essential for both mother and child. For the infant, the weaning is essential to his reaching the stage of development suited to his age and capacities; for the mother, it is essential in connection with her regular family and community life. Regardless of how strong and positive her attachment to her baby may be, it is natural and proper that she resume her participation in kibbutz life. She is helped by the maternity benefit norms, by the fact that she has a regular place of work, and by the knowledge that an understanding metapelet is in charge of her baby and his group while she is at work.

Gradual weaning also helps in the formation of a link between the baby and the metapelet, who assumes a significant role in its life, and in eliminating "eating problems."

After the weaning is completed, in addition to the usual time spent with her child or children in the afternoon, the mother will stop by during her morning or noontime break.

Later in the day, the baby is taken to his parents' quarters until bedtime, when they bring him back to the babies' house and put him to bed. (This is customary until the age of 12 to 18 months.) If difficulties arise in the baby's parting from his parents, the metapelet stays nearby to soothe him, give him a toy to take to bed, or put him on the floor to play for a while.

A kibbutz-reared infant becomes aware of the other children in his group at a very early age. He lives in the same room and sees them in their beds close to his own. Later he eats with them—first on his mother's lap and then at a table—and together they crawl about the floor. Sometimes, when the metapelet wants to comfort a crying baby, she puts one of his peers into bed with him. (Naturally, she must also closely observe the relations between them—these may take an aggressive turn.)

For the infant, the babies' home is the first stage in the formation of the *kvutza* (the educational group); for his parents, it is the first stage in their link with the parents' group—the initial step on the road to collective education. In time, these relations become increasingly strong and firm.

The reader may well gather that the babies' house is a true home, both for infant and parents. Here the mother experiences intimate encounters with her baby as she nurses him. Here, at his bedside, she shares with her husband the joys and anxieties of watching their child develop. And here, too, in the babies' home, the extended family (grandparents and siblings) also gathers frequently.

The role of the metapelet is important. Newborn babies, who require the highest level of care, are put into her experienced hands. She must be alert to everything that happens, day and night. At the same time, the mother enjoys a wide range of initiative and freedom of action, and can behave with her baby in a manner suited to her own aptitudes and character. Based on her professional understanding of and sensitivity to all possible mother-infant relations, the metapelet carefully resists any suppression of natural feelings between mother and baby. She fulfills her educational, social, and practical role in close collaboration with the mother, a partnership that has inestimable value for the young child.

The babies' home is the organized expression of the kibbutz's concern. Its staff strives, with a high degree of success, for as little turnover as possible. This factor, conjoined with the successful application of principles of baby care and education, has yielded a minimal infant mortality rate. Pioneering doctors have worked out routines of baby care and feeding that are most suited to Israel's difficult climatic conditions. The attractive design and arrangement of babies' homes in most kibbutzim is the outcome of a vast accumulation of practical experience on the part of the metapelet.

The children's houses, the children's community, the accommodations designed specifically to correspond to their physical capacities, the games, and the attention given to their needs—all these constitute the "child's world," which begins in the babies' home. Thanks to the care and love bestowed by their families and by the kibbutz community as a whole, the children grow up secure.

The Toddlers' House

When kibbutz infants reach the age of one, they are moved into the toddlers' house *(pe'uton)*. These more spacious quarters provide toys, a play area, and other amenities geared to their physical development and potentialities. The group of four or six toddlers leaves the babies' house as a unit, and moves into the *pe'uton*, where they will stay until they are ready for kindergarten.

Ideally, the metapelet who has known the child from birth should remain with him for the first three years of his life. However, this is not always possible—for example, not every metapelet can readily adapt to toddlers; also, a metapelet must sometimes leave for personal reasons: pregnancy, health, or another assignment. For these reasons, at the age of 18 months the child is turned over to another metapelet. But she has already had a period of contact and training with her future charges in the babies' home and has come to know each child.

We have found that the optimum educational setting from 18 months to three or four years old is a unit of four to six children with one permanent metapelet. A well-trained metapelet can devote the necessary time and attention that ensures the maximal development of each child. The small-group arrangement promotes the formation of those emotional ties which are basic to a profound relationship and to the identification that is such a positive feature of the kibbutz system. Within such a framework, constructive educational demands can be made of each child. The metapelet's confidence in and love for each child, and her influence as an educator, are decisive at this stage, when the relationships among the children—their social development—are being molded.

The toddlers' group helps the small child to accept the demands of reality put to him by the metapelet. The very fact that these demands (e.g., interrupting a play period for a meal or for bedtime) are put to *all* children in the group makes it easier for the individual child to accept them, for he is naturally inclined to identify with and imitate the behavior of his peers. The demand does not turn into a direct conflict between the child and the metapelet; it is the accepted way of life in the toddlers' house. This does not mean that there are no difficulties over such matters; however, the element of deep-rooted conflict with the adult is eliminated.

At the age of three, the group begins to merge with another of the same age, in order to lay the foundations for a new group of eight to twelve children. Both metaplot work in close cooperation for several months, bringing the children together for some activities while maintaining separate groups for others. This period of mutual adjustment, when relationships are formed between children in both groups, prevents the ultimate merger from coming as a surprise or shock. Instead, it is a natural and organic continuation of their group life, preparations for which have been made well in advance.

Those in charge of toddlers (ages one to four) assume an enormous responsibility, for it is an age characterized by strong expressions of feeling: the child is torn by conflicts between his instinctual drives, on the one hand, and the educational environment and its adult representatives on the other. It is also a period of rapid and interesting physical, emotional, and spiritual growth.

In the past, some erroneous attitudes concerning this age group resulted in errors in handling them. Today, even though we now have a better understanding and knowledge of the child's world at this age, we constantly seek to study and improve our methods, aided both by scientific advances throughout the world and by our own experience.

The appearance and layout of the children's house—the grounds, the facilities, the style—exert a profound and decisive influence, aesthetically, socially, and culturally. The house is not merely a place where the child spends his time or where he is cared for. He lives there most of the day and night; he is completely attached to it; his bed is his world; he loves his own corner. The house is warm and pleasant; it feels good to be there. His parents, too, should sense the warmth radiated here, so that they can feel absolutely confident that it is the *right* place for their child. The homelike, intimate atmosphere has an important educational value for children and parents alike.

Every arrangement in the house is geared to the small child. It is inadvisable to have sharply demarcated sections, such as bedrooms, washrooms, dining rooms, and playrooms, all separated from each other. The entire house should be easily accessible to the child. In every corner he will find what he requires, commensurate with his developmental level: furniture, toys, pictures. Toys, games, and play material, in our opinion, are important instruments in fostering spiritual, mental, emotional, social, and motor development at this age. Through them the child develops his senses, dexterity, and movement; through them he also expresses his feelings. In the absence of such equipment, his life would be barren and tedious, lacking the stimuli that are so vital for self-expression, activity, and creativeness.

The same criteria apply to the grounds surrounding the house, which we regard as the natural extension of the home and where the youngsters spend many hours each day during the long summer months. The spacious grounds—well-fenced, yet open, with trees to provide shade and with different activity areas (a sandbox, water taps, and crates with all kinds of "treasures")—form their own world, expanding the area of the child's activity and enriching the possibilities for play and creativity.

Daily Routine

The daily routine for toddlers is adapted to their physical development and to their capacity for activity. We divide the small child's day into two parts, with a midday rest period. However, as we have pointed out, the children are not left on their own in the house. A metapelet is there during rest hours, too.

The metapelet begins her work in the children's home in the morning, before the children wake up. When the children are between 12 and 21 months, there is also a morning rest. However, consideration is given the fact that some older children need a rest period or an extra hour's sleep in the morning.

Following is an example of the summer schedule:

6:00-7:00 A.M.	Arise; dress
7:30	Breakfast
After breakfast	Free play out of doors (while the house is being cleaned)
8:30-10:30	A walk, play, and other activities; work in the garden; a fruit snack
10:30-11:30	Showers and water play
11:30-12:00	Lunch
12:00-1:00 P.M.	Nap

1:30-4:30	Free time for the permanent metapelet (she is replaced by *another metapelet* at this time); free play for children indoors
4:30	Light snack
5:30-8:30	Visiting period with parents
8:30	Supper, bedtime (the children are put to bed by the metapelet)

The above schedule is only a general outline; changes may be introduced to correspond to the needs of the children or their parents, as well as to regional climatic conditions.

The winter schedule is somewhat different; for example, they get up later and go to sleep earlier; other activities (including walks) are arranged in accordance with weather conditions.

Persons Who Influence the Child's Development

The kibbutz educational system has proved that the presence of several *permanent* individuals with whom the child can identify in his early years exerts no negative influence on normal development; in fact, it is a positive factor. We are not alone in holding this view.

In the long run, everything depends on the social significance attached to the various individuals. In the kibbutz, the metapelet is not an outsider, in the same way that persons who are not members of the immediate family are not considered strangers and relations with them can be close ones. According to Margaret Mead, research into various "primitive" cultural environments has shown that adaptation is far easier when the child is looked after by a large number of warm-hearted and friendly individuals. Kibbutz education would seem to confirm the validity of this premise even in a modern society, and herein lies our most important contribution to the science of contemporary psychology.

In the first year of life, a process vital to the development of the personality takes place. We refer to the process of "the child's incipient discernment of the ego as distinct from the non-ego." In his first months of life, the infant has no sense of self: he does not differentiate between himself and other persons or objects. His "ego" sense is not yet fully developed, since he is still incapable of sensing the boundaries of his own body. The child begins to make this distinction in the second half of his first year—a process that is closely connected to his growing capacity to recognize other people, his physical surroundings, and the various individuals in his environment.

Identification and Identity

When the baby's emotional equilibrium is upset by bodily needs—hunger, thirst, pain, excessive warmth or cold, etc.—he becomes aware of his dependence upon reality, upon the essential, real objects that alone can satisfy his needs and restore equilibrium.

The baby's link with reality develops with the help of those looking after him—particularly his mother, who feeds him. It is she who satisfies his primary biological need. He learns to recognize her through his senses — sight, touch, smell, etc.—and by the way in which she satisfies his needs. When she is not near him, his sense of security can be assured only through the emotional attachment built up from his past experience with her. This emotional attachment is actually identification. From this we may conclude that the beginnings of a feeling of self-identification are determined by two factors: (1) a dependence upon reality and the satisfaction of primary needs (in the human child, in particular, this is *not* something that happens instinctually); (2) an identification with the person who satisfies these needs.

This identification does not take place in a vacuum. It is dependent upon the satisfaction of the baby's physical needs, the most important of which is hunger. There are other needs, of course, such as that for bodily contact and closeness, which stimulate the nervous system and the senses. The older persons's concern for the health of the infant, for his warmth and clothing, and for other aspects of baby care is expressed in a flow of feeling toward the baby, and from the child back to the adult. These emotional channels are varied and manifold.

An infant's feeling of security depends upon the prompt, regular, and unfailing gratification of his needs whenever they arise. One individual alone cannot possibly fulfill all these needs adequately, as every mother who has raised a child in the kibbutz will confirm. Greater success is assured when the mother and the permanent metapelet work together to create an environment that will afford the infant many forms of contact. He thrives in a world that is devoted to him, a world continuously providing for all his needs and winning his confidence. The fact that the baby forms an emotional attachment to more than one person helps him to identify with the individuals in his environment and, by stimulating his feeling of self-identity, increases his self-confidence and feelings of independence.

The premise that a single object of identification is the main guarantee—indeed, almost a necessity—for the development of strong personality needs and a strong ego would seem to be unfounded. In fact, it appears to us that the existence of a single person as an object of identification is a fiction, the result of a quasi-scientific invention that is divorced from reality. Even within the accepted framework of family upbringing, the child has more than one person with whom to identify—the father, siblings, a grandmother, aunts, possibly a governess—all, or some of whom, participate actively in taking care of him.

The Positive Value of Two Persons as Objects of Identification

What is the situation in the kibbutz babies' home? The child's emotional attachment to his mother, and his identification with her, grow from their mutual contact as she nurses and cares for him in his early months of life. The baby is as sensitive to the exaggerated love often expressed by a mother as he is to a paucity of love. He expresses this in crying and restlessness, just as his calmness conveys satisfaction with the measure of love bestowed. There are no fixed "measures of love" equally valid for all babies; this is a variable, dependent on the physical, psychological, and environmental factors affecting both mother and baby. We have no control over many of these factors, and where the child shows a lack of calm and contentment—occasionally or most of the time—the fact that the metapelet is on hand to play her part in caring for him serves as a balancing factor to reassure the mother and the infant. This has been our experience in connection with all aspects of feeding, weaning, and hygiene.

The entire process of education is, *inter alia*, a progressive series of severances—beginning with the period of total dependence in early infancy and continuing until the attainment of adult independence. The child copes with the crises of severance by identifying with the loved objects with which he must loosen or sever his ties. The existence of other objects of identification (the child does not have to sever his ties with every object at the same time) helps and comforts him through each difficult period.

The advantages of the processes of identification with both mother and metapelet lie in the fact that they are not subject to simultaneous removal from the child's immediate world and, in any event, not with equal impact. For example, when the process of weaning is at its height, regular contact with the metapelet is maintained. And at all times, even when the child is experiencing the crisis of accepting a new metapelet, the link of identification with the mother remains firm. Those who fail to recognize the many-faceted nature of the baby's attachments to every person in his environment overlook the fact that he is attached to the surrounding world in its entirety, and not to his mother alone.

In the early months of life, the baby does not identify with several persons in the sense of being able to distinguish clearly between them. It may, however, be assumed that the image of the individual who takes care of him, as the infant absorbs it into his personality, is a combined one, consisting of elements of both the mother *and* the metapelet. By the time the infant learns to distinguish clearly between the mother and the metapelet as two real, entirely distinct individuals, he will already have comprehended the different nature of the attitudes and relations between each of them and himself. The mother is uniquely *his own* even before he can articulate this verbally.

It may be assumed that the concept of a "stranger" is radically different for a baby in the kibbutz than what it would be in a strictly family-based urban community. In the kibbutz, an identification with several persons from the time of his birth is characteristic of the collective way of life he will experience in the future. The kibbutz community is composed of friends and acquaintances, a situation that is very different from the social-psychological realities confronting the city child. It is against this background that the identification of the infant in the kibbutz babies' home should be considered. It is irrelevant to ask, "Whom does the child call when he is in difficulty—his mother or the metapelet?" In our society, he may call either one, depending on the circumstances.

In the first year of life, there is no such thing as identification with the mother-figure as the person who looks after the infant—neither in the kibbutz nor in the case of individual family upbringing. The difference lies in the fact that, in the kibbutz educational system, an organized social attempt has been made to define distinct spheres of activity for the various adults involved and to ensure effective cooperation between them by integrating their activities.

We see the following advantages in the presence of several figures in the baby's life: there is a reasonable division of baby-care functions, which eases the crises of severance from the loved objects at successive stages of development; habit training can be more patient and straightforward than is often the case when the mother alone is responsible; the infant is instilled with such a basic confidence in the people surrounding him that the word "stranger" assumes an entirely different meaning and usually loses any connotation of fear; and the infant's links with his peers create stimulating interpersonal relations that intensify his feeling of self-identity and give him an added sense of security.

It should not be assumed that the multiplicity of figures involved in the care of the infant should be allowed to develop into a haphazard or unstable situation, or that frequent staff turnover should be tolerated. On the contrary, regular periods spent with parents, a permanent meta-pelet, and a permanent group of children, as well as stability in the routines of the baby home, are prerequisites for the sound interweaving of all the objects of identification into the fabric of a stable environment.

The toddlers' home setting, and the special relationship that develops both within the group and between the group and its metapelet, help the children to cope with various tensions that may have accumulated in the family and in the surrounding world. This is manifested in dramatic play or in conversation among themselves. Here is a conversation between four-year-olds who have just been put to bed, as written down by their metapelet:

Shai: Alon, did you know . . . ?

Anat: Have you forgotten, Shai? You're not supposed to talk to Alon, because I'm your neighbor. . . .

Shai: Do you know what I saw? I saw Yoram—not your father, Gil, another Yoram, Yoram our neighbor. He took the bulldozer.

Gil: My father's tractor?

Shai: Your father is night-watchman.

Gil: No, he isn't; today he went to town.

Shai: Do you know, the tractor broke down; they didn't see it at all.

Gil: Well, it can be pulled out of the mud.

Shai: With a "bugger"?

Gil: No, with a crane.

Alon: A crane can lift things and a "bugger" can't. A bull-dozer can push things and a crane can lift them up.

Shai: Do you know what happened yesterday? The bulldozer called out to the State of Israel and the Egyptians made war. And I made clowns for them. Clowns with pistols. (All laugh.)

Anat: Was that nice?

Shai: Yes, it was. When the Egyptians came, they took the "Shmar-taf"* and took out a wall.

Anat: Did they come to the State of Israel? That's not allowed!!!

Gil: Nasser was the commander of the war.

Anat: No, he wasn't, only of the Egyptians. Our commander was Rabi.

Shai: Not Rabi—Rabin, like that. Rabin lives in Hadera and I'm going to bring him here from Hadera [the town closest to the kibbutz] —our commander.

Anat: Do you think all the farmers went to war, and only my daddy stayed behind in the kibbutz? Were they angry at him?

Shai: Anybody who's got a day off doesn't go off to war.

Anat: My daddy once went to war for five weeks.

Shai: My dad went ten times.

Anat: Mine went a hundred.

Shai: A hundred is terribly little.

Gil: The Egyptians have nothing and we have cotton and potatoes; they've got nothing at all.

Shai: The Egyptians have a well. . . .

(At this point the conversation ended, and a few moments later all was quiet.)

Conversations of this kind take place frequently when the children are in bed and before they drop off to sleep. The metapelet always stays nearby until they have fallen asleep. She listens to their conversations and takes part in them when necessary. The conversations provide important material for the staff, indicating directions to take in their educational work. They also give the metapelet an inside view of the child's world and of the problems occurring in it.

Education of the "Ego"

Many educational, psychological, and social aspects are involved in harnessing the young child's instinctual drives. Over the years, collective

*An intercom which enables one woman on night duty to handle several homes. The children are trained to talk at the "mike" if in need. The sound of crying also reaches the woman on duty, and a flashing light indicates where she is needed.

education has passed through several phases of development, with corresponding changes in attitude toward the interaction and interdependence of various aspects. Our past experience has been taken into account in the development of our theory regarding the optimum methods of habit training and the channeling of instinctual drives. We continually seek to appraise our methods in terms of our basic doctrines and guidelines.

What are the principal phases in the development of collective education, and what were the stages of its crystallization?

In the earliest phase, we took a strict approach to habit training—a heritage of the authoritarian view of education. Later, a conscious effort was made to break from this view: in practice, if not in theory, no demands were made on the child. In the third phase we achieved a consolidation of educational methods, and the psychoanalytic theory of the "ego" was taken into consideration.

Those responsible for formulating the directives of kibbutz education endeavored, above all, to introduce progressive ideas into the struggle against formal authority and against the attitude which held the small child to be an "object" for education rather than a person in his own right. This phase can be described in the following terms:

> The phenomena in the child's behavior which accompany his growth (such as thumb-sucking, infantile masturbation, etc.) are manifestations of natural psychological forces. They are therefore termed "instinctual" to denote that these are not "bad habits" which must be severely prohibited and uprooted, as is maintained by traditional pedagogy. We regard them as manifestations of psychological phenomena which we should seek to divert into educational channels. Education of the instincts does not mean bringing them *mechanically* under control but, rather, *refining* them without total repression of their *gratification*. It is our educational objective to train the little "savage" to take his place in the civilized community, while repressing his instinctual activity as minimally as possible.

Considerable emphasis has been placed here on the social-organizational aspects of kibbutz life, for it is these which lend significance to familiarity with psychological principles. The fact that the children are housed together, away from the intimate lives of their parents; the arrangements for putting the children to bed; the division of educational functions between parents and staff—all this imparts to the education of instinctual drives a special, distinct value. The guiding principle in our approach to pedagogical explanation has become the requirement that the channelling of instinctual drives should not be a technical or mechanical matter, a question of merely curbing these urges and of repeated practice, but should be a process of psychological development. The *principal* requirement of educational workers is not that they suppress instinctual urges; instead, they should induce sublimatory activity. The struggle against overstrictness, against the legacy of a repression-motivated past, was at the core of this development in our educational attitudes.

In the course of time, a further refinement occurred. Full recognition was accorded to the system of collective education for its great contribution in the cementing of kibbutz society. In educational-psychological terms, after World War II the ideas of the psychology of the "ego" strongly penetrated our way of thinking. Although educational-psychological views regarding the channelling of instinctual drives and their decisive role in the molding of the personality prevailed, this was now supplemented by added knowledge of how these drives could be adequally utilized for the purpose of shaping the personality. The crystallization of educational demands in infancy and early childhood now proceeded with the stimulation of psychological understanding and with our cumulative experience. Today, we consider the strengthening of the child's "ego"—for example, cultivating his senses, increasing his motor aptitudes, and understanding and improving his mental processes—the principal and most effective means of directing his instinctual drives into constructive social and human channels. While we do not overlook the fundamental impact of these drives, we do not hold them to be primal forces over which man can exercise no control. An educational path has thus evolved, the most outstanding characteristic of which is a positive reaction to the instinctual drive. The channel of these drives has, in fact, become the education of the "ego."

We endeavor to create conditions for the child that will allow him freedom of movement and creative activity. In this connection we seek methods that correspond to the needs of his sensory pattern, his developmental level, his motor capacity, and his cerebral ability. These aptitudes enable the child to utilize his psychic energy in a sublimative manner. For this reason we believe that children should acquire the experience of community living from their earliest days—both as a means and a vital framework for the process of socialization.

Kibbutz education advocates tolerance toward manifestations of instinctual drives, and attains its educational goals without resorting to pressure, threat, or repression. Kibbutz education is perhaps the only setting which, as a comprehensive public education system, has been guided by this principle, and whose results have proved the validity of one of the major hypotheses of modern psychology. This may be regarded as a unique contribution of the kibbutz educational approach to the contemporary sciences of education and educational psychology.

the kingergarten . . . affords many opportunities for self-expression

The Kindergarten

by Miriam Roth

A kindergarten group of 15 to 18 children lives in its own house, which has bedrooms, a playroom, a dining room, and an outdoor playground with suitable equipment. The kindergarten is formed by combining three groups of three-to four-year-olds. They remain in the kindergarten for three years and have the same teachers.

As the children approach the ages of four to five, their capacity for community life grows and, with it, the scope of their activity. They express themselves through the use of all kinds of materials and through group activity involving movement, music, and dramatic play. The size of the group allows for the formation of many-faceted friendships—some permanent, others casual. We also find here a dynamic setting for the formation of subgroups in which the roles of the leader and of the led, the initiator and the individual activated by others, are interchangeable and can be exchanged dramatically and rapidly. The collective life, its varied activities, the very essence of the kindergarten and of the child-

35

ren's home, all create a framework for practice in social living. The young child learns the nature of social give-and-take; his image of himself changes in accordance with his ability to participate in the vibrant life surrounding him; and he gets to know where his own talents and abilities lie while he learns from friends who are better informed than himself.

Permanent educators are assigned to the children throughout the day. They reduce the tension so often found in this age group by directing activity into positive channels.

The children are involved not only in the usual kindergarten program, but in taking care of the house, the garden, the grounds, and pets. Under the surveillance of their teachers and in accordance with their abilities, they also help with cleaning and tidying up, with the distribution of clothes, or with washing dishes and cleaning shoes. This gives them practice in sorting, in fitting things together, in measuring sizes, and in reading signs and names. The children enjoy working with the teacher (as one six-year-old put it, "I'm helping you to wash dishes because I like talking to you"). Such activity also develops a feeling of mutual responsibility and strengthens a sense of belonging to the house in which they live. A child who makes a contribution to the improvement of his group's home feels that his own importance has increased.

Other kibbutz institutions are involved in the kindergarten daily routine. When the seasons change and summer clothing has to be turned in, the kibbutz sewing center and the shoe store become centers of interest for a few days. In the excitement of receiving a new item of clothing, new shoes, or rubber boots—a joyous experience for every child the world over—the kibbutz child comes to the workshop he knows so well and to the people he has known all his life. They tell how the articles are made, they show him the materials and the tools used, and the way in which the work is organized. All this exposes the child to opportunities for independent activity and for an organized experience in the broader kibbutz setting. The world of their own concepts expands as they come into contact with the broader environment and learn about the connections between different elements in the material world and the human world. Common group experiences serve as a background for group links with a genuine content and for stimulating activity around new topics.

A lively group life, and learning through group experience, help to wean the children from infantile dependence upon their parents; to some extent, this facilitates an equilibrium in the turbulent emotional relations with parents that are so characteristic of this age. The relationships formed between the children and the kindergarten teacher and metapelet are also of an emotional nature, but they are stimulated by a common interest that is varied and adapted to the child's needs, and therefore serve as models for links between the children and other adults.

The Parents' Home

A group of 15 to 18 children allows for a considerable range of experience in social living. The kindergarten home responds to the needs of the growing child, emotionally and intellectually, while enabling him to develop his relationships with his parents and to form his personality.

More than anything else, it is the parents' home that constitutes the decisive emotional center. The main family meeting takes place at the parents' quarters after work, when tea and a snack are shared by the entire family. Each person, coming from his job, brings something of interest to share with the others. The child participates in preparing the tea or in looking after a younger brother or sister. He sometimes works in the garden or performs a household chore. He calls his parents' house "my room."

The relations between parents and children are usually warm and friendly, for their encounters are based more on shared, *pleasurable* interest than on parental demands or on the fulfillment of duties (which sometimes lead to conflicts). The parents' influence helps the efforts of the group's educators; the latter, in turn, counsel some parents in connection with educational and psychological problems. Most of our parents are alert to problems of child development and usually cooperate with the staff to learn new approaches to child-rearing.

The late-afternoon family meeting is not the only visit. Parents frequently visit the kindergarten before work. Also, if their work on the kibbutz grounds is close enough, the children stop by—sometimes alone, at other times with children from their group or with their teacher.

The parents' strong links with the children's group involve them in its everyday life. They can observe their own child and his behavior within the group; they can share the reactions of those in charge of his education; they are invited to special events and help in preparing for holidays and other occasions; and they work on projects for the kindergarten house—for example, building equipment for the playground, sewing costumes for dolls or for the Purim carnival, etc. Such involvement strengthens the child's feeling that his children's home also belongs to his parents, and that his parents' home and his home are not separate authorities but are linked to each other in the same society. From this stems the deep significance of the word "ours," which even small children use: "our vineyard," "our sheep pen."

The proximity of the children's home to the parents' quarters, conjoined with the social proximity of the parents and educators, creates a rare situation: the educational workers see the child in the context of his family and can sense any change in his behavior; the parents, in turn, can evaluate how the educational workers are doing their job. These factors create an integrated setting for collaboration between the various educational components, and increase the prospects for a harmonious influence.

Celebration of Holidays

An outstanding example of the children's participation in the molding of cultural patterns is the celebration of holidays. The kindergarten house takes on a special appearance as each festival approaches. The children help in the preparation of food associated with the occasion; they use traditional symbols to decorate every corner of the house, including a spot next to each child's bed and even in the pet corner on the grounds. Holiday preparations are important: the celebration becomes not merely a casual event, but represents the culmination of a varied process directed toward one special happening.

Every holiday has its own perceptual associations: colors, smells, flavors, sights, and sounds. Even a relatively minor custom or ritual repeated every year takes on a special value. A small girl once summed up her "impressions" of the festivals as follows: "Hanukka is the festival of silver and gold; Tu B'Shvat [the spring tree-planting festival] is a festival of green, Purim [the spring carnival commemorating the story of Esther] is multicolored; May 1st is red; the festival of harvesting the first fruits [Succoth] is yellow—from the corn-sheaves in the summer field."

The purpose of every tangible holiday symbol is to consolidate its particular background in the child's heart. The child *likes* holidays, looks forward to them, and experiences them as part of his life. The seasonal rhythm of the festivals, each at its appointed time, brings joy to his heart. The world that is revealed to him in its festive garb instills the aspiration to be part of it, to belong to it.

In this lively and dynamic setting, full of love and joy, we build our first "explanations" of the significance of each festival, its place in the past and the present, in accordance with the intellectual capacity of the kindergarten child.

Activities in the Kindergarten

The kindergarten child's timetable has considerable elements of diversity. The children are awakened at a fixed time (varying with the seasons), but not in military fashion. Some jump up early, others like to stay in bed a little longer; but as soon as a child is up, he begins his active life in some corner of the house. Breakfast is taken by all the children together; those who rise first help in its preparation. Before breakfast the children gather for a talk, a short walk, or gymnastics. The morning is devoted to intensive activity—partly individual creative and play activities and partly joint activity organized by the teacher. After lunch the children shower and rest, and are then free to play until it is time to visit their parents. They are brought back in the evening by their parents, and then go to bed.

The kibbutz kindergarten house is organized as a setting for individual activity. The prime need of the kindergarten-age child for creative self-expression through the use of materials and through play is satisfied in varied ways:

A group of boys gather in the bricks corner. They build a ship from large hollow bricks and, using toy trucks, transfer the cargo from the truck to the ship's hold. One child suggests constructing a crane and, under his guidance, the children look for suitable materials to carry out this complicated task. A chair is put on the table; wheels from a construction set, and wire provided by the kindergarten teacher at the children's request, make for an excellent crane. The child whose suggestion it was celebrates his success; he becomes the "commander" in charge of loading and unloading. The game proceeds—until the "captain" remembers that a radio is required. The children close off the bottom of the "boat." One child goes into the hollow space formed by the bricks, and from there he hums tunes and broadcasts messages—he is the ship's radio operator and "loudspeaker" at one and the same time—and everyone listens to the "program." The voice on the radio invites the girls to get on board (they have been busy in the doll corner). The girls dress up like ladies, carrying suitcases and handbags, hats on their heads, parcels and dolls under their arms. Theirs is the role of passengers, and the game now involves the entire group.

Here we have characteristic play with wide possibilities for choosing satisfactory roles, motivated by the inner need to identify with adult characters. The social roles of the children change with dramatic speed: at one point in the game the sole leader is the "captain"; at another time, the "crane operator" assumes the leading role; later, the "radio operator" takes over, followed by the girls (and their presence changes the whole tone of the game).

This particular game raises "scientific-technical" problems that require immediate solution so that the enthusiasm engendered can be maintained. The solutions, based on the children's own conceptions, express the knowledge they have acquired on the subject from their own experience (the crane goes up and down when a rope tied to a wheel raises or lowers the cargo; the radio is thought to be closed from the inside, where a person sings or talks, etc.).

I have described a game characteristic of a group of children whose repeated visits to a port have broadened their experience. In other kindergartens the games differ—depending on the experience of the group—but a common feature is that they always serve as the arena for a pattern of social relationships, for experience in leading and in being led. The games create a wide field for the expression of feelings, they raise problems, and they enable solutions to be found in accordance with the intellectual level of the children. Alert to these potentialities, our staff sees to it that the play corner has an abundance of varied material, including items that are relevant to the experiences encountered in the outside world and can serve as a stage for the dramatic presentation of real events. The house is so arranged that the children can work with creative materials at all times of the day (most kindergartens have a workshop next to the playroom, where chalk, paints, glue and paper, as well as wood, carpentry tools, and other materials are available).

In selecting the different materials and using them to express their desires and interests—in their own way and in accordance with each child's stage of development—creative activity can be conducted in a helpful atmosphere. The teacher's appreciation of each child's attempts at craftsmanship is expressed by encouragement in words and by the fact that every creative effort, no matter in what form, is preserved. In this way the child can see his own progress; he develops an attachment to the forms of self-expression that are characteristic for him, and achieves a refinement in his mode of expression.

We were confronted by the problem of whether four- to seven-year-olds are capable of spending so many hours together. Although the kindergartener is quite sociable, he also displays considerable intensity and, occasionally, dramatic and exhausting tension. His abilities and strength are growing, and he seeks his own identity. Play groups form and disintegrate in rapid succession, and the child must adapt to varying situations: sometimes he is the group leader, while on other occasions he plays a minor role.

The layout of the kindergarten home (and of the grounds) is instrumental in reducing social tension. Well-arranged play corners in each bedroom and in the yard make it possible to hide, to seek solitude, until he is ready to join in the formation of a play group. The kindergarten house affords many opportunities for self-expression, so that the child can adapt his powers to the tasks which he sets himself and which he carries out with the help of his peers.

The Kindergarten Staff

The fact that the kindergarten teacher and the metapelet are permanent and that they are devoted to their work is decisive in determining the atmosphere in the kindergarten. The overall routine and regulations are based on the children's capacities, and help to instill a sense of security as well as of freedom. The teacher is responsible for the general program, for enriching the content of the children's life, and for their many-faceted development. In addition, she participates in their physical care and takes her meals with them. The metapelet participates in trips, in the preparation and celebration of holidays, etc. The educational staff in every phase of kibbutz life has come to realize that the kindergarten teacher and metapelet have an equal impact—both in creating a correct atmosphere in the house and in shaping the child's personality and consolidating the group as a whole.

The children can distinguish between the tasks of the teacher and those of the metapelet, but they also sense the unity in their duties. The greater the harmony in approach and outlook between those in charge, the more aware the children are of the importance of each. They feel free to discuss questions of dress, food, illness, etc., with the teacher, while they also involve the metapelet in the events connected with the life of the kindergarten.

Uri runs from room to room, looking for the metapelet to show her the drawings he has just completed.

Netta declares in the morning: "Today we are going for a long walk. Come on, let's help Shifra [the metapelet] to tidy up the house so she can come with us."

This kind of cooperation between metapelet and kindergarten teacher requires regular communication: they must consult each other with respect to a particular child or the group, there must be harmony in their "credo" on education and on other questions, and they must understand the activity of children, the value of self-expression, the relationship to parents, etc. Such cooperation requires not only a high level of training, but regular refresher courses to deepen their knowledge. We are mindful of the need not to be complacent, but to increase our efforts in this connection.

In a prekindergarten setting, the metapelet strives, through warmth and affection, to create in the young child a feeling of security, belonging, and closeness. But the functions of the kindergarten staff assume additional dimensions: the children see them as a source of information and knowledge, they turn to them for help with group difficulties and social rules, and they see in them an example of moral and well-mannered behavior. The staff is a bridge between the adult world and the kindergarten group, and in the eyes of the children represents society and its values. Together with the children's parents, the staff represents the kibbutz society and conveys the complexity of that society to the children.

The kibbutz, a democratic society, requires that the relations between children and their educators, from the early years on, be of a democratic nature. Mutual respect must be based on mutual appreciation, and not on formal authority.

Emotional Problems

The kibbutz kindergarten is not merely a house where the child lives, eats, sleeps, and struggles for a position in the group—it is also an emotional focus for the children and for their parents.

Even though the children do not live with their parents, they are very sensitive to anything that affects their relations with them. A son's competition for his mother's love manifests itself in various ways, and prompts him to identify with different male roles in the kibbutz environment. The girls also seek sexual identity by fulfilling "motherly" tasks (they help with cleaning up, with preparing meals and clothing, etc.) and by lively, dramatic play in which they can act out their hidden desires. The staff has many opportunities to observe the family relations during the daily visits. In offering guidance, the educator does not *criticize* the approach of the parents, nor does she accuse them in any way; but her advice on how to spend the shared time can in many cases add new content to family relations.

> Uri's father—a tough man who tends to authoritarianism—prompts both fear and rebellion in the child. The daily conflict in the parents' quarters begins the moment Uri asks to use his father's work tools and the latter refuses. Both "men" are obstinate. The mother intervenes, helping the son to insist on his right to the tools; at the same time she comforts and cuddles him. Uri returns, ill-tempered, to the kindergarten. He is angry with his father and prefers the gentleness of his mother. But after he leaves his parents, he begins to cry and wants to "tell Daddy something."

A talk between the educators and the parents will certainly not alter the deep, subconscious factors in the family relationships, but a few practical suggestions on how to change the way the family's time together is spent can diminish the competition and create a feeling that Uri is a "man" and not a baby who needs his mother's comforting, thereby helping to improve the pattern of family relations. The counseling is always geared to the particular circumstances, to the changes in the development of the kindergarten group, and to the changes in the child.

The children bring their problems from the parents' home to the children's home—strained relations between child and parents, or between a child and his siblings, are projected. The relations between the child and his educators allow him to transfer turbulent feelings from the family to the kindergarten, and from the kindergarten to the family. *The reactions of the educational staff to outbursts of anger and to emotional tantrums are more objective than at home. This gives the child many opportunities to put to the test a sensitivity different from what he has come to know at home. In experiencing different reacting patterns, the dimensions of his conduct toward others are altered.* In the case just cited, the child's obduracy encounters the obduracy of his father and the spoiling attitude of his mother, but these are counterbalanced by the friendly and restrained attitude of the kindergarten teacher. Here we have simple and convenient opportunities for reeducation.

Manifestations of jealousy between siblings are also transferred from the family to the kindergarten. The social behavior of one child can reveal his strivings in the family circle: he "adopts" a brother (from among the other children) whom it is easy to dominate or in whose shade he can seek shelter. Another child finds a "victim," a target, for his concerns (the birth of a sibling, a death, separation, etc.). The educators *know* the children well, and that fact in itself *ensures an individualized approach.*

The kindergarten equipment and an atmosphere that encourages activity allows a wide scope for self-expression via clay-modeling, painting, mud and water play, dramatic play, and dance. In this way they "free" themselves from what oppresses them, while "revealing" themselves and their problems to their educators and "helping" them to find the right approach to solve them.

When a child requires special attention for persistent fear, over-aggression, speech difficulties, etc., a staff member takes the child under her wing. She gives him individualized attention, the main purpose of which is to gain his confidence and determine what is troubling him. The way she handles the problem differs according to the child and his tendencies. Some children express themselves best in words and describe their dreams; others prefer to draw; another type of child plays with "his miniature life toys" and acts out his situation. This is by no means psychiatric treatment; it simply makes it possible to extend the child's self-expression, to provide him with individual attention from people who are close to him and whom he likes. The group is healthier if its individual members are healthier and more balanced. The group is richer if each individual is capable of developing his individuality and achieving self-fulfillment. Only by knowing every child—his tendencies, fears, and aspirations—and by cultivating him and meeting his individual needs can we achieve all these goals.

First Grade (the "Interim" Year)

The kibbutz kindergarten includes the *first grade*—six-year-olds who begin to learn reading and writing in a rich environment. *Creativity* and *play* at this age reach a high level, and are utilized by the child not only for self-expression but as a challenge to learning, scientific experiment, and discovery. In their games, the children re-enact *whole chapters of life,* introduce clear rules of behavior, and apply the cultural patterns they have already absorbed. The group becomes increasingly more united around matters of common interest, and can express its approach to actual events in the environment.

In the course of this year, the children manifest a growing interest in reading, writing, and arithmetic, all of which fit in well with their rich pattern of life. Learning is not conducted in a formal manner. A *reading corner* is added to the various corners in the kindergarten house; there the children find relevant material—reflecting their present level of interest and written by the kindergarten teacher—in booklets or on decoratively arranged reading boards. *The arithmetic corner* has instruments and materials for exercises and illustration, and offers wide scope for individual and guided exercises. The teaching of reading and writing is centered around meaningful *projects* drawn from the immediate environment; they are sometimes suggested by the children and involve all kinds of experiences. (No textbooks are used in teaching reading and writing, because the contents of the books available do not fully convey the essence of the life of kibbutz children. Consequently, material prepared by the kindergarten teacher is used.)

The community life of six- to seven-year-olds develops the ability for mutual help and the aspiration for autonomy. The children learn, from repeated experience, that many projects can be carried out only by pooling their resources, and that the community can accomplish things which one individual cannot do on his own. There are interesting group enterprises, as yet childish in content, but the main trend is to stress the child's ability to be independent and to work through the initiative of the group, with minimum intervention on the part of the adults. The children organize parties and produce plays; in "troubadour" fashion, they visit other houses to perform their plays for younger children. The awareness that they possess the ability and power to influence the course of life in the kindergarten heightens their desire to learn.

At this age, active links with the adult world are also strengthened by contact with adults in various sectors of the kibbutz economy. Such attachments are sometimes astonishing in their intensity. Here is an example:

> A group of children learned about the dairy farm and spent a lot of time walking around the cowshed. The cowherds described their work and soon developed close ties with the children. The children's knowledge was supplemented by booklets and posters written by their teacher. When the project was almost completed, the children insisted on organizing a party in the cowshed "because of the pleasant smell there." They wrote out invitations to the people who worked there, cleaned up the place, and undertook the responsibility for the organization and program of the party.

The "interim year" offers the children a rich variety of kindergarten experiences—an opportunity for self-expression that allows for more social independence and for learning through doing—while at the same time preparing them for school life.

The Kibbutz Society

As the child's motor-physical capacities increase, he reaches every corner of the kibbutz and forms ties with those working in his surroundings. There are times when he is free to walk by himself or with a group of friends—without adult supervision—either to places where special-interest activities are under way or to a hiding spot for secret games. Every nook and cranny becomes familiar, a challenge to investigate and seek new knowledge. The children develop close emotional ties with every tree, every rock, every inch of ground, at the same time familiarizing themselves with everything that transpires on the kibbutz grounds. They are the first to announce that the combines are being readied for the harvest or that a new truck has arrived, that a calf was born or chickens have been hatched in the breeders. The children's stories about what they themselves have witnessed are of special interest to everyone. Sometimes the others in the kindergarten group and the teachers are summoned to a new "discovery."

One of our objectives is that the links established during childhood will also constitute a permanent foundation in adult life. The educational means and the educational goal are interdependent, and both are linked to the kibbutz in which the children form their childhood attachments and where they will be reared and will work.

A child's deep attachments to adults help in the formation of the personality. Children are sensitive to the cares of adults and to their joy in success; they wholeheartedly share the feelings conveyed by adults about problems that concern them. This identification increases their feeling of belonging, of self-knowledge, and of power.

> The children enthusiastically relate that "our" dairy farm has succeeded in achieving a record yield and has been awarded an efficiency prize: *We* have succeeded." They share in the success, proud that they belong to the adult group which did so well.
>
> When rain is expected, the youngsters anxiously look up at the sky and declare in all seriousness: "May it be granted that there be no drought this year." Sometimes they don't quite know what is meant by "drought" or what a drought year

implies. But they sense the depth of concern felt by the adults, and realize that by sharing this worry they are becoming an organic part of those who are so troubled.

The activity program in the kindergarten is based on what goes on in the kibbutz society. At the height of the season, when many adults work in the farm sector, children sense the excitement and share in it.

The children visit the vineyard several times during the grape harvest. They examine the fruit, distinguishing between the early and late varieties. They hear explanations by the vineyard workers; they lend a hand in picking and packing the fruit, and in sticking labels on the crates. The intensive work seen in the vineyards, involving many adults, is an important influence on the children. In sharing the work, their feeling of participation is enhanced. And no experience is more exciting than having breakfast with the workers in the vineyard shed.

The children bring back interesting "finds" from their trips, and assign them to various special corners: plants and insects go to the nature corner; fruits and vegetables are delivered to the kitchen corner, where preserves will be prepared, raisins dried, and fruit juices made. The work of the kibbutz is linked with the activities of the kindergarten; in turn, the scope of the kindergarten expands, reaching out to the kibbutz limits.

Participation in kibbutz festivals is an unforgettable experience. The child sees familiar adults in their best clothing, joining in community singing, dancing, and artistic performances. The youngsters can feel the importance of the festival by observing the attitude of adults.

A mother of several children, who was herself born in a kibbutz, recalls:

I shall never forget the picture of the *haverim* dancing, the way I saw it for the first time. I was five years old. Father stood me up on a bench. During the festive meal I had sat next to him but couldn't see the hundreds who were eating together. Then, suddenly, the circles of dancers appeared before my eyes— singing softly, first slowly, then quickening their pace, and dancing, first slowly, then quickly. . . . And all so beautiful, so new. . . . I turned to my father enthusiastically. "Everyone in a white shirt!" I exclaimed over and over again, unable to stop repeating the same words because my heart was so full and I could find no other words to express my feelings. . . .

satisfaction from working and playing with children his own age

The Junior Children's Community

by Hava Shamir

The junior children's community encompasses the years known as late childhood—from eight to twelve years of age. It consists of four educational groups: the third, fourth, fifth, and sixth grades (the third grade is admitted in the last term of the school year). Since each grade is a social-educational unit limited to 15 or 20 children of the same age, this makes individualized care and instruction possible. At this age, too, the children require a wider and more varied choice of companions for play and friendship, a requirement that is met within the broader framework of the children's community.

Youngsters of this age have a vital need for a group and for finding their place in it. They generally form themselves into groups led by an older child. The groups tend to be secretive in nature, with established patterns of obligatory symbols, codes, and rules. As Stone and Church (1965) point out, this phenomenon of forming groups is common in many societies; the child's need to express his growing self-assurance, his

49

independence of the adult world, finds an outlet within the peer group.

The peer group—the *hevra*, as the kibbutz child calls it—seeks channels and goals through which to express independence, energy, and initiative. Through its work for a common objective, the "gang" consolidates and acquires a meaningful existence—unlike the experience in the West, where gangs often display negative and antisocial behavior and even degenerate into criminality. On the basis of our experience, we have concluded that while the tendency to form groups at this age is a real and vital need, the antisocial content of these groups is not. If the child is offered a wide range of activities in a democratic atmosphere, he will find positive goals and channels through which to express his independence and there will be no need for negative group manifestations.

Our children's community provides suitable conditions for independent social activity, varied and rich in content and appropriate for the specific age group. Its aims, which are of a *positive* nature, are not directed *against* the society but, on the contrary, work toward strengthening ties with it.

The children's community affords each child the opportunity to derive satisfaction from working and playing with children his own age. Enriched social experiences contribute to a happy childhood. The gratification derived from positive social contacts may well prove a source of self-confidence, which, in turn, promises a healthy socialization. His activities with others, his successes, and his confrontations with wishes that are opposed to his own will help him not only to understand the behavior of his peers but to gain insight into the mechanism of his own behavior.

Socialization and Individualization

Members of the children's community spend most of their time in the company of other children. While that is a natural tendency at this age, some environmental conditions may blur the individual characteristics of each child. His desire for acceptance by his friends may hamper the expression of his own ideas and attitudes. This type of pressure is found in every age group, but in the kibbutz framework, where the educational system encompasses the child's entire day, it may well do harm to individual development.

How do we attempt to cope with this phenomenon? We encourage every initiative to form small, mixed-age groups (8-10 or 10-12) which set positive goals for themselves. A small group of this kind, which is based on friendship and strives to fulfill a concrete objective, goes through a crystallization process. From its very formation, every individual can and should contribute, according to his ability, to the attainment of the set goal.

The tendency to conform, so typical for this age, can be modified by alternating the centers around which this crystallization occurs. A group of this kind generally breaks up once its purpose has been fulfilled, and opportunities for new centers are created. In addition, the educator sought out by the children encourages them to express their ideas freely and to give due consideration to the issues at stake.

In small groups the child has the opportunity not only to accept the leadership of a companion but to assume the role of leader, since the alternation of centers of activity also paves the way for the individual to change his status in the group. In terms of content and implementation, the group activities are varied: preparation of plays, investigation of various branches of the farm, inquiry into natural phenomena that arouse curiosity, care of animals, organization of a sports day, construction of hiding places in treetops, growing flowers and vegetables, organizing a camping outing or a chess tournament, etc. A child who is particularly adept at field cooking is not necessarily skillful as a playwright or stage designer. The boy who regularly carries off the sports trophy does not always display competence or conscientiousness when looking after chickens or leading a discussion in the children's community.

When individuals are chosen for various kinds of activity, the children are well aware of each other's talents and how to best utilize them. We try to provide the conditions for an exchange of functions and for changes of status within the groups, so that everyone is given the opportunity to prove his own abilities. It should be kept in mind that even though the children acquire many intellectual, cultural, and artistic values in the course of extracurricular group work, this is not the main goal. The aims of such activity are to make allowances for differences in abilities and interests, to utilize special talents, to develop cooperation, and, most of all, to provide channels of independent, creative work.

The Attitude Toward the Adult World of Parents and Kibbutz Members

The authority of the kibbutz educator is not taken for granted, as is the case in the conventional school. Relations between the educator and the children are primarily based on guidance and cooperation rather than on external control and unquestioned authority.

The nature of these relations is a function of the overall relations in the kibbutz society. Both the educational workers and the parents are representatives of that society and implement its principles in their lives. The pattern of relationships, as the children see it, can be expressed as follows: "Parents, together with other kibbutz members, form a community whose deeds and goals I respect. In the future I want to act as they do!"

The characteristics of the child at this stage of his development enable the children's community to function as a major factor in socialization. The child is confronted with demands for social and civilized conduct, since most of his needs are satisfied within the framework of the children's house.

Even though it may seem that parents have no specific educational duties, they are actually the most permanent and influential of the various figures with whom the child identifies. Some parents tend to have incorrect notions about their role: they pamper and indulge a child instead of supporting the demands of society, as a result of which the impact of these demands is diminished. Morever, when an imbalance develops in this subtle fabric of child-parent relationships—in which love, demands, and support are interwoven—the child's attitude toward his parents is also impaired. The integration of parents into the process of defining educational goals, as well as guidance to them about their meaningful role as parents, seems to us to be of utmost importance.

How the Junior Children's Society Functions

The Children's Farm

The children grow up in the kibbutz, the mainstay of whose economy is a large, ultra-modern farm with thousands of chickens, hundreds of dairy cows, and thousands of dunams [one dunam equals about one-fourth of an acre] of field crops and orchards.

Why, then, do they need a farm of their own? A large, highly mechanized farm, where everything is done on an enormous scale, is too complex for the child. He cannot find his way around it or understand the laws governing it, nor can he influence or direct it in any way. On the small children's farm, however, he himself can determine many things. Here his dedication, his aspiration for independence, find expression—for example, he becomes attached to a certain animal and sees the progress and results of his devoted care.

The children's farm is fenced in and surrounded by trees. Inside we find a duck pond, a dovecote on a tree, and coops with various fowl. In another corner there are rabbits in underground runs, two goats, three sheep and, of course, a donkey for riding and for pulling the farm cart (on the big farm, work animals are a thing of the past, having been replaced by tractors and trucks). The proud peacocks spread their tails and look down contemptuously at the male turkey as he does a clumsy courting dance before the lady of his choice. Every morning, in all kinds of weather—rain or a burning hot sun—the children can be seen delivering leftovers for the chickens in their cart, going out to cut green fodder for the animals, cleaning up in and around the cages. The size of the cart, of the tools, and of the cages is suitable for the children. They work for one hour in mixed groups, two or three from each class. The older children assume responsibility and show the younger ones what to do, while the youngest ones—the third graders—are proud to do the job of feeding the chickens, goats, and doves.

An important factor is the staff member who accompanies each team, not only for practical guidance in work and in caring for the animals, but in helping the children to persevere in carrying out their tasks. There tends to be a considerable gap, in this age group, between the actual and the desired capacity for assuming responsibility. The satisfaction derived from achieving the goals he has set for himself encourages the child's initiative and his willingness to assume new responsibilities.

The children's farm, like most activities in the children's community, functions on *two levels*: (1) an organized level, based on a definite pattern, and (2) a spontaneous, independently organized level.

Organized Activity: The children elect a farm committee from among their own community; it serves for three months and is guided by a staff member. Together with an adult from the kibbutz, the committee draws up a plan of priorities for the jobs to be done, such as repairing the cages, paving a new path, or fixing the roof of the barn. It supervises all jobs, decides whether ducks or chickens should be raised, and suggests names for the new animals born or acquired. The committee also discusses suggestions made by children at a group meeting and, once approved, sees to their implementation. The children's farm earns income from the sale of birds and eggs, and the children's community makes budgetary decisions (based on committee proposals) as to whether the money should be used for buying animals or for other purposes.

Spontaneous Activity: Here is an example of spontaneous, independently organized activity: The grandfather of one boy is a farmer at Nahalal, a moshav [cooperative village]. He offered to give us turkey chicks, which must be grown in winter. These sensitive birds cannot live without heat, but there is no heating installation on the children's farm. The request was passed on to the farm committee, which presented it to the general meeting of the children's community. It was proposed that a group be formed within two days to find ways of solving the problem of how to look after the chicks.

The group, consisting of six children, made a detailed plan: how the chicks would be brought, where they would be housed, and who would look after them and how. The general meeting approved the proposal, which called for fourth and fifth graders to be in charge. Their tasks included preparing a warm hay bedding for the day-old chicks, finding out about proper nutrition and providing it, bringing oil stoves to the breeder shed, and seeing to it that everyone on night-watchman duty kept the stoves filled and burning on cold nights.

The chicks were weighed once a week, and the results published. Once the "special treatment" was completed, the chicks were transferred to the children's farm. The group summed up its projects with the educator-counselor (these evaluation discussions after the completion of a project are of considerable value in the social education of the children).

The small-group framework makes it possible for every child to make a contribution, both in suggesting ideas and in implementing a project. Such a group frequently lays the foundation for new friendships that continue long after the completion of the project. Sometimes the same group works on several successive projects.

By setting valid goals and providing proper conditions for carrying them out, we attempt to satisfy the child's needs during this stage of his development. Activities of a distinct social nature draw the children closer to the social patterns of the adult community.

Other committees in the children's community function in the same way: the Library Committee, the Secretariat, the Jewish National Fund Committee, and the Social Affairs and Sports Committees, all of which form the institutional aspect of the group's social life. Since they function according to familiar patterns, the children are easily able to run them.

The Library Committee

The job of the Library Committee is to take care of library books and catalog them. An adult staff member is in charge of the library, but the children wrap each book and suggest reading material to library users. They are also responsible for the library bulletin board, which displays propaganda about books that are not so popular at the moment, as well as reports on the books read by the children. The ideas in the material on display are expressed naively, dryly, or as propaganda, depending upon the child who wrote the report. Later, some of the reports are selected, edited, and included in the library catalog, and this proves to be helpful to the library management.

A special Library Committee project is the Book Festival, where groups present extracts from books they have read and have chosen to dramatize.

A Book Evening

The Library Committee conducts a referendum to elect the annual King of Books (the last vestige of monarchy in our country!). Prior to the event, the committee sponsors discussions on the merits of the books "crowned" in the past, and draws up a list from which the children can choose one for presentation. The initiative now shifts to the children, who divide themselves into groups that generally reflect friendship or similar talents. Then they choose the book they wish to present.

In such a group, which has been formed for an artistic purpose, the status of each child is assessed according to a new criterion: those with a flair for writing and producing plays, for designing sets and costumes, and for writing lyrics now have a chance to display their particular skills.

Once such a group is consolidated, a sense of identification with its goals and with the other members quickly develops. Here, too, the group assumes the characteristics of the classic "gang." Secrecy reigns over the selection of the book, the nature of the play, the preparation of the costumes and decor, and the site of the group rehearsals. Every group member shares a feeling of mutual responsibility (no one would dream of revealing the gang's secrets, and everyone tries in every way to cooperate so that the common enterprise is a success), and each individual is loyal to his group. Every year the staff tries in vain to persuade the children to do without this secrecy in order to reduce the tension!

A staff member is assigned to each group; he helps and guides the children when asked to do so, and acts as moderator if difficulties arise. It is desirable for the child to engage in independent activities that inspire creative imagination, but it is also important for him to have recourse to an adult if he wants advice.

After two weeks of preparation, usually during school holidays, the annual party takes place. Dressed up, made up, and excited, the children gather in their meeting center, which has been decorated with drawings about their favorite books. In the audience are their parents and the second graders who are too young to have been a part of the preparations.

A committee of judges is elected—adults who have no direct links with the performing groups and who are neither parents nor educators. The children deliberate at length about the criteria to be taken into account: should the quality of the acting or the play itself be the decisive factor, or should it be the decor and costumes or perhaps the literary value? Finally, a list of points is drawn up for the judges to consider in weighing each performance.

The book festival concludes with the awarding of a prize to each group: cakes or a treat.

The Community Newspaper

Each issue of the children's community newspaper is devoted to a specific topic: their farm, some interesting sites in the district, sports, social activities, bird-watching, etc. The Editorial Committee announces the subject, and a group of "journalists" write the articles or encourage others to do so. Illustrations accompany the articles, and the final products are hung on the walls of the clubroom. Sometimes one of the articles triggers a debate or a public referendum.

Group Meetings

The group meeting is the highest body of the children's community; it determines rules of behavior and makes decisions concerning the major issues facing the children. What should be done with the money left over in the farm till? Should farm animals be sold, or new ones purchased? How should games be organized so that the weaker children will not be discriminated against on the playing field? Other questions concern how best to organize the time after the formal entertainment at a party so that everyone has fun; how to divide the children's community for a forthcoming trip—in separate groups or in one large group; how to make sure that librarians are not the only ones privileged to have first access to new books; and how to organize the break between lessons so that some children do not return late to class.

The entire educational staff participates in this type of meeting, which is directed by the children except for the first part known as "a quarter-hour of urgent business," which is chaired by the counselor-teacher. During this first period the children propose topics which have not been included in the agenda, but which they believe to be of great importance. These newly raised issues give the meeting an urgent and vital character. They involve such matters as fairness and priorities, discrimination in various forms, the social pressures to which the child is subjected and with which he tries to get along, etc. Suddenly the children discover that it is possible to put such feelings into words, that there is nothing to be ashamed of, that they can talk about problems in a civilized manner and even seek ways of solving them.

Here are some items that are raised in "quarter-hours of urgent business":

> "Our gang got together and started to build a hut up in a tree. We have two boys and three girls in our group. The older boys are teasing our two boys about having secrets with girls."
>
> "We have a certain secret, and other children keep following us to find out what it is. Are they allowed to follow us—what are the rights of the gang?"
>
> "The metaplot insist that we refrain from playing football in our best white Sabbath clothes. Are they right?"
>
> "I lost a library book, and the librarian insists that I must find it before I can take out another book. Is it my fault that the book was lost?"
>
> "The teachers insist that we come on time to supper. But how are we to know the time? Are we supposed to sit and watch the clock instead of playing?"
>
> "Is it all right to choose teams before all the children have reached the playground?"

Some of the issues are dealt with on the spot; others are referred to the "clarification group." An announcement is made: "Today we are going to clarify the issue of the rights of the gang. Anyone interested in participating should submit his name." A group of six to eight children of varying ages is chosen for the clarification group, together with the educator. It is easier to clarify matters in a small group. There is time to listen, to consider all arguments. Through such a discussion, concepts and demands become more clearly defined and a certain objectivization takes place.

The solutions are sometimes brought to the entire children's community for review. If they are accepted by all the children as binding, a *tradition* is established. The children's identification with a community tradition, one which they themselves have created and formulated, is intensive and genuine.

In the democratic society in which the kibbutz child is destined to live, it is essential that every individual know how to examine issues and arrive at conclusions, for a kibbutz member is continually called upon to cast his vote on various matters. That is why we attempt to *involve* the children in molding the norms of behavior in their community; they learn to understand the rules of society and to identify with them, while simultaneously strengthening their inner discipline.

The children are not capable of considering and deciding every issue. Some matters are beyond their authority—e.g., the hours for study and sleep, safety precautions, the type of film showings they can attend, and meal arrangements. The staff decides these matters, but since the adults acknowledge the children's rights and respect their decisions, the youngsters do not regard these limitations on their authority as unfair.

We believe that consistent adherence to a set definition of the children's sphere of authority has great educational value. A child's confusion increases and his self-confidence is undermined when responsibilities and decisions for which he is not yet ready are heaped upon him. When an issue does call for a decision by the children, adults must be willing to abide by it. Even when we are anxious about their decisions, we must help in carrying them out without trying to affect the results in any way.

Education cannot take place in the absence of discipline and norms of behavior. The familiar helps to offset confusion and to instill confidence in the child. The established norm serves as a criterion for behavior, while discipline preserves the stability of social contents. The decisive factor in the children's community is the manner in which its norms are established.

Highlight of the Year: The Camping Trip

Once a year, at the beginning of the spring holiday, the children's community sets out for a day of camping. The planning and execution are entirely in the hands of the children, without any help or participation on the part of adults.

Lengthy staff deliberations were required before the first such event. Is it not too great a responsibility, we asked, for the children to choose the groups by themselves? After all, the more capable children might group together, leaving the weaker ones to fend for themselves. Then, too, some children might be left out altogether, particularly the less

The Project Method: Elementary Schools

by Lea Alterman

The educational methods in kibbutz schools evolved both within the context of the social aims of the kibbutz movement and as an outgrowth of Western progressive educational trends in the early twentieth century. How did these separate developments combine to form the kibbutz approach to education?

The kibbutz represents an attempt to create a society of equality and democracy of the highest order, a society in which there is no power structure. It aspires to achieve human relations based on lofty humanist ideals, and its culture attempts to foster the multilateral development of the personality within the framework of the needs and goals of kibbutz society as a whole. It is not surprising, therefore, that the founders of this movement were attracted to the ideas of progressive education, the essence of which is the development of the child's personality and the stimulation and channeling of his inner forces.

The kibbutz movement adopted the fundamental ideas of progressive education, namely, that childhood is an age with its own rights and that there is a need for the development and refinement of the child's "inner forces" rather than for their suppression. This approach maintains, too, that education should be based upon psychological research.

We shall attempt here to describe the present method of education for children of elementary school age (seven to twelve), methods which were nurtured in kibbutz soil, which drew upon the ideas of progressive education, and which were altered and developed by everyday life.

Principles of the Project Method

The project method, a system of educational instruction, embodies two main characteristics: (1) it bases the curriculum and teaching methods on the developmental needs of children and on the maturation of their mental and psychological aptitudes, adjusting to the individual requirements of each child; (2) it does not regard the imparting of knowledge as its sole purpose, but uses this as a springboard for the education of the child's personality.

These principles are proclaimed in the introduction to every teaching program. The difference, however, is that the project method does not content itself with a mere affirmation of such comprehensive aims, but puts them into actual practice through its instructional means and didactic methods. Let us first enumerate the chief characteristics of the method, and then describe their application in the school:

1. The content and method of teaching are planned so as to enable the children to take a genuine interest in what they are learning and to stimulate their activity.

2. Learning is conducted within the group as a social activity, under the guidance of the teacher-counselor, who gives support, shows understanding, and acts in a democratic spirit. The teacher encourages initiative and independence in the pupils.

3. The instructional methods are varied, but emphasis is always placed on the pupil's *individual work.*

4. The capabilities, inclinations, and aptitudes of the individual child are constantly borne in mind by the teacher.

5. The purpose of the curriculum is to inculcate knowledge and develop intellectual capacities and manual skills, with emphasis placed on certain attitudes and values: humanism; attachment to the Jewish people, to the country, and to our national heritage; re-

spect for work and for the working man; a striving for social reform; an esthetic sense; and a striving for knowledge and the ability to use it in the personal fulfillment of these values within the kibbutz.

6. The curriculum does not comprise a number of entirely separate subjects, but is a totality of "life-units." The child learns to understand concepts in their relationship to life, in the way they are rooted in reality, and to apply them in different contexts.

7. Learning methods provide opportunities for social contact and discussion, educate the children to be considerate of others and foster team work.

8. Given the *educational* principles on which the project method bases its teaching, there is no need to make learning a matter of coercion and competition. Instead, the aspiration for achievement in learning and in group life is stimulated in the child.

We shall now analyze in greater detail some of the fundamental principles on which the project method is based and cite several illustrations of how they are applied.

Learning motivated by genuine interest and active participation. This, in a nutshell, is the main principle of the project method.

We shall briefly review some of the origins of this approach in the history of educational theory, how it has been applied and developed under the project method, and the changes that have been introduced.

At the beginning of the present century, when progressive education began to flourish in Europe and the United States, the principle of interest-motivated learning, involving the active participation of the child, was advocated. Outstanding educational theorists declared that "it doesn't matter *what* the child learns—the main thing is that he should enjoy learning it." This extreme viewpoint can be better understood as a reaction to the traditional educational system at that time, a system under which teaching meant education for discipline and self-control, based on the principle, so to speak, that "it doesn't matter what the child learns—the main thing is that he should hate his schooling." This new school of thought influenced kibbutz education to some degree, but the greatest impact was made by the educational theories of John Dewey and his followers.

The educational philosophy that influenced educators in the kibbutz movement at the outset may be summed up as follows: The wish to learn is an inborn instinct; the urge for contact with the environment and adjustment to it are characteristic of every living creature. Learning is a process that takes place through the child's contact with his environment, a contact he strives for. The child, therefore, has an instinctive desire for knowledge, but this instinct may be distorted by faulty methods of teaching. The school should base its activity on the substance of the actual life style of the child's environment. However, learning cannot be allowed to take its own course; the teacher should focus the children's attention on problems that emanate from their own environment, problems whose solution can be found by the children only through their acquisition of knowledge and the development of their thought processes.

When confronted with a problem, a child will want to do something to acquaint himself with a field of activity; he will try to achieve results and, in order to do so, he will have to think, learn, and add to his stock of knowledge. All the purposes of learning—the acquisition of knowledge, the development of the capacity to think, and the attainment of physical skills—can be achieved through the method of confronting the child with an actual life experience.

The teacher does not come to his class and announce, "Today let us study the caterpillars that are destroying the cabbage plants." Instead, the children themselves say, "The cabbage leaves in our garden are being eaten up; what are we going to do about it? We have to find out why, and learn about plant pests—and save our garden!" That is how knowledge, practical skills, and the ability to discern causality—the essence of logical thought—are acquired.

In the conventional school, subjects are taught as bodies of knowledge organized according to a specific inner logic—a logic resulting from the adult's view of a world divided into separate subjects. Enlightened teachers try to stimulate interest in these subjects through didactic means, whereas others are content with trying to instill them in the child mechanically. In the progressive school, however, the actual learning is itself of significance; it has purpose that is vital to the child. In the conventional school, the child learns chapters from his textbooks; in the progressive school, he has at his disposal reference books in which he can seek the information he needs for a purpose recognized and desired by him. To help attain his purpose, he also acquires knowledge by observation, experimentation, contact and discussion with others, and other means. The success of learning is assured, provided that it stimulates the interest of the children and gives them scope for activity.

The above-mentioned principles constitute the basis of the project method, although they have been somewhat adapted in their implementation. One must keep in mind that the actual forms of this method are not completely established; as in any other progressive school of thought, they are still undergoing changes. These changes result from

of the area determine its source of income: the farm's branches, its security (distance from the border, etc.), sources of water, and so on. Thus, in the course of the project, the children will leave their own kibbutz and also take into account the entire area, including all the neighboring kibbutzim.

In the following year, as fifth graders, the children will work on another project whose subject is the geography of Israel. This will familiarize them with a particular region where the landscape, the economic resources, the sources of livelihood, and even the way of life of its villages are different. They will discover much that is familiar to them from their previous work, but they will also find many new elements.

Equipped with fundamental knowledge and concepts, the child will now be capable of absorbing and understanding the differences between the two regions. In this system of learning, the teacher-counselors accompany their pupils for four or five days and nights to the new region, spending 24 hours at one of the cooperative villages (moshavim) in order to experience living with people whose way of life is entirely different from what they have been accustomed to all their lives.

The moshav is an agricultural settlement based on many elements of cooperation, but profits, consumption, and the education of children are a matter for the individual, and the principles of equality are practiced differently than in the kibbutz. During their visit the children are put up in the homes of villagers and spend one day attending classes at the local school. They participate in the work of the family in the early morning hours, and get to know the family's farm, which is much smaller than the farm unit in the kibbutz.

Before they set out on the study tour, they are asked to "guess" what public institutions would be required by the residents of the moshav, what they are likely to find in the village center, and how the villagers' farm, the moshav school, and its institutions are organized. Once the children have become aware of the fundamental differences in the organization of these two forms of village life, they will be able to apply their formerly acquired knowledge and distinguish to what extent the organizational patterns of the kibbutz would be suitable to the moshav way of life. The advance classroom preparation sharpens the children's discernment of what they will encounter and heightens their curiosity and awareness. In addition, they study the map of the region before the visit, and try to conjure up a picture of the crops, the industries, the transportation, the exploitation of water resources, the regional purchasing centers, etc. They also draw up a series of questions to ask their moshav hosts.

In the sixth grade, the children study an urban center, which they also visit, spending five or six days there. This time, too, they will acquire new knowledge that will dovetail with or supplement previously mastered concepts.

As the children get to know new ways of life (in a moshav, in a town), emphasis is placed upon understanding and evaluating the differences between them, and between them and the kibbutz. Powers of judgment are developed. By integrating the familiar elements with new spheres of learning, the need for repetition and review becomes superfluous. This is how previously acquired concepts and knowledge are applied anew at each stage of learning, and become an instrument for understanding the new reality being encountered.

We will now present several projects undertaken in different grades. The program of projects for every grade is suited to the scope of interest of the children of that age group, and aims at achieving the skill and knowledge that are consonant with the ability of the children and with educational requirements.

The general curriculum of the school is a single educational program covering the *first six years of schooling*. It was elaborated in the course of many years by the educational staff of the elementary schools in Kibbutz Artzi. The staff closely follows the day-to-day educational process by means of lengthy deliberations and then by generalizations.

The curriculum, though now crystallized, is not a hard-and-fast one. Flexible and subject to change, it is continually being reconstructed around the living child. The teacher, rather than being confined by the curriculum, uses it as a loom on which to weave his own educational patterns.

The Annual Program of Projects

In the lower grades (ages seven to eight) it is not difficult to include in one project all the aspects of study and fields of knowledge which the children require, both for the present and as preparation for future stages of learning. Beginning with the fourth year of school, however, and particularly in the fifth and sixth grades, the achievements in theoretical study required of the pupils are more closely defined, and it is no longer possible to include in every project every field of study and to place the necessary emphasis upon each. In these grades, each project is based on one or several main areas of study—each of which is accompanied by skills, handicrafts, and creative means of expression—while the curriculum of projects for the entire year is designed so as to preserve a proper balance.

The fourth and fifth grade projects are described in Tables 1 and 2.

TABLE 1

Fourth Grade Projects

Project Name	*Subjects*
THE CITRUS OR OLIVE GROWTH	Botany; study of the environment and of the life of the inhabitants; history of the settlement and of its culture; map drawing, agriculture, concepts in the economy of the country; connection with ancient history (the olive is frequently mentioned in the Bible and other literary sources).
OUR KIBBUTZ AND ITS ENVIRONMENT	Study of the economic and social organization of the kibbutz, or the ideals motivating it. Agriculture and basic concepts in the economy. Origin of its members; "merger of the exiles" (a fundamental precept in Israeli policy of integrating various sections of the population, regardless of country and culture of origin); the beginnings of Zionist pioneering in Palestine; forms of settlements in Israel. Study of the environment, present and past. Map drawing. Geography of Israel.
FIRE	Study of matter and its properties; natural physical phenomena and the laws to which they are subject; work processes; citizenship; the beginnings of civilization.
FROM SLAVERY TO FREEDOM	The Bible—Book of Exodus. The aims of teaching the Bible in the elementary school are: (1) to impart concepts and symbols of

the spiritual world of ancient Israel; (2) to create an attachment to the national leaders and heroes and to the nation's history; (3) to extend the bond with the land of Israel and thus foster the development of a world of greater dimensions in the children's concept of "homeland"; (4) to cultivate the imaginative and conceptual abilities of the child and enrich his knowledge of the Hebrew language; (5) to give the child a literary-artistic education by experiencing the classic literary creations of ancient Israel.

ROADS AND TRANSPORTATION

Study of matter and its properties; the work process; civil organization, familiarity with the environment; map drawing and reading; the geography of Israel.

THE BIRD POPULATION

Zoology; influence of the environment on the bird's way of life; the structure of bird population; study of the surroundings and of the landscape.

TABLE 2

Fifth Grade Projects

FIELD AND GARDEN

Botany; zoology; agriculture; concepts in general economics and the economy of Israel; the beginnings of agriculture.

FROM A TRIBE TO A PEOPLE

The Bible—First and Second Books of Samuel.

THE MIDDLE EAST

Physical, economic, and political geography; study of the ethnic groups in Israel; getting to know the Arab village in Israel. Civic organization.

HAIFA AND ITS ENVIRONS (OR TEL AVIV OR JERUSALEM)	Geography of Israel; landscape and climate in different districts; study of the city, its past and development. Concepts in economics and the economy of Israel; the state and its citizens. History of the settlement of Israel.
THE ANCIENT EAST	Ancient history; geography; the history of civilization.

As regards the projects, the following observations should be borne in mind:

1. In the list of subjects incorporated in the projects, we have not included the Hebrew language, literature, and mathematics. These are included in almost every project; the way in which they are incorporated will be discussed in greater detail below.

2. The arts are also part of every project, since the objectives of instruction include the fostering of esthetic appreciation and enjoyment, as well as the encouragement of creative expression through painting, pottery, decorative work, dramatic presentation, music, and dance. Within the context of all projects, a great deal of time is spent on handicrafts, a form of creative expression that is most suited to childhood years. However, their principal value is that they involve *activity*—a most important aspect of learning. Different handicraft tasks are undertaken for different purposes: *illustration and modeling* (for example, building a kennel or a poultry run; casting bricks; making relief maps in a sandbox; making a compass); *creative handicrafts* (reliefs; pottery; cutouts and paste-work in paper and other materials; decorating, cutting out, etc.); and *making objects from various materials* (a notebook, a bookmark, a decorative box, basket weaving, embroidery). All three types of handicraft are involved in every project, and the child generally makes them an integral part of his work.

3. Every project provides opportunities for education in certain attitudes, outlooks, and values. In some cases this opportunity is inherent in the actual content of the project itself: love for the kibbutz surroundings, identification with personalities in the nation's past, sympathy for the fate of the suffering, and good citizenship. Important educational goals can also be realized through the methods of working on the project, methods that foster initiative, independence, a desire for knowledge,

understanding of one's fellow and respect for his individuality, and the ability to work in a team.

4. It is sometimes asked how it is possible to ensure that the children's learning is based on genuine interest—after all, they are not given the opportunity to choose subjects that are specified in advance in a planned curriculum. As we have stated, the project method attempts to integrate the child's learning in accordance with his own interest and with the objective requirements of education and knowledge. To achieve the latter, the project must be planned and carefully designed so as to include graded spheres of learning.

Can a teacher occasionally adapt such a project to fit in with the choice of the pupil? Today, teachers have at their disposal many study projects which have been worked out by experienced educators and are included in the curriculum. Our experience has shown that children look forward to these projects because each generation of children tells its younger brothers and sisters of the intriguing aspects of a particular project, thereby enhancing its attractiveness. But this is not enough. It must be borne in mind that choice enriches and stimulates the sense of independence that is virtually an elixir of life for the child and a vital impetus to his desire to learn. It is therefore desirable to give children the opportunity to choose between several projects that have been planned in advance, or, from time to time, to initiate a new project. The central teaching team currently favors two or three alternatives for each project theme (as shown in the tables) and encourages initiative in developing new projects.

In addition, there is also the possibility of "teaching by opportunity"—that is, if the children are moved to curiosity by some outstanding public or social event or by some rare natural phenomenon, the teacher may switch from the current project and deal with the phenomenon that has aroused the children's interest. Here are several examples:

1. A comet was due to become visible in the night sky; it could be seen clearly only at 3:30 A.M. Comets cannot possibly serve as the central theme around which a study project can organically be woven, but this phenomenon was of the greatest interest to everyone in the kibbutz and was the talk of the day.

   At 3:30 A.M. we awakened the children and, accompanied by a kibbutz member well versed in astronomy, went outdoors. As the children observed the night sky, they were told what a comet is and the many superstitions that have come to be associated with it. As dawn broke, the bright color of the comet began to fade, and slowly its glowing tail vanished. This experience was followed by classroom study of books containing legends and stories about comets and the stars.

Some of the children spent their time reading and studying about famous comets of the past, while others looked for pictures and snapshots illustrating the subject, wrote captions with the proper dates, drew pictures recording the event, or wrote stories about their impressions. Finally, the illustrations, poems, stories, and descriptions were collected for a wall newspaper, and other classes, as well as parents, were invited to see the results.

With this, the impromptu project was at an end: it had a short life, and no attempt was made to go into the subject in any depth, since we did not feel that it contained extensive possibilities for study suitable for this age group.

2. A butterfly resembling what is hatched from the silkworm laid eggs on the curtain of our classroom. The female insect was weak—she seemed hardly alive—and the process of laying the eggs continued for several hours. We were in the middle of a project, but it was clear that we could not ignore an event that was actually taking place in the classroom, especially since it was autumn, when these butterflies are particularly rare. This was indeed an extremely unusual event. The children looked in nature books and encyclopedias for information on the life of the butterfly. They counted the eggs, collected them, and put them in a suitable place; they set out to discover the best way to look after the growing caterpillars, and prepared a small cage. Every evening they went out to catch more butterflies. They discovered a male of the same species and studied the differences, learning to distinguish between the male and the female; in this connection they remembered what they had learned about insect life in the previous school year, during a project on ants. They also brought back caterpillars of the same species and fed them.

While the female was laying her eggs, the children could not take their eyes off this fascinating sight—it aroused their keenest curiosity. This led to a short inquiry into insect life, their adaptation to conditions of life, their enemies, etc. A dramatic event of this kind, rooted in nature, is most suitable as a brief impromptu project. It occupied us for three days. We also visited a natural history museum in the district, where the children saw collections of cocoons and various species of butterflies. On the third eve-

ning, parents were invited to hear the children report on what
they had observed, and a filmstrip on butterfly life was shown.

It should be noted that if the occasional topic is likely to supply
enough material of interest to occupy the class for a longer time, and if it
contains educational and cultural potentials that are suitable for the age
group, the teacher interrupts the original project and weaves a new pattern of learning around the subject that attracted the children's interest.

To sum up, the projects recommended in any syllabus cannot possibly
convey the actual learning activity, which is linked by a thousand invis-
ible threads to the landscape, to the specific society, and to the various
events in the life of the child. No syllabus can possibly convey the
liveliness of childhood—the questioning, the imagining, the puzzling, the
unexpected initiative, the susceptibility to unforeseen impressions, the
activity and play, and the way children constantly learn.

The Integration of Subjects

As we have already pointed out, the project method has done away
with conventionally separate "subjects." Several subjects are coordinated
within the same project, either because they are actually different aspects
of the same life-unit or because it is necessary to learn them in order to
solve the problem posed by the project.

For example, the central theme, "The Citrus Grove," requires studying tree growth and cultivation, and varieties of fruit, and the pests that
harm them. Since it is also relevant to determine when citrus cultivation
first began in the country, this leads to the history of the first Jewish
villages. There is research into the origin of the citrus fruit and its distribution, which involves aspects of geography and the history of civilization. The economic viability of the citrus economy is also of interest
to the children; here, of course, arithmetic is relevant—both study and
exercises. Naturally, there is no child who would not be attracted by the
idea of walking in the kibbutz citrus groves with a compass and a map.
The setting for this project is the actual citrus grove of their own kibbutz, where their parents and other kibbutz members whom they know
so well are working. They bring back fruit and specimens of insect pests
from the orange grove for classroom study, and they go out to help
pick the fruit and look after the trees.

In the fourth grade, the children study *citrus fruit* or the *olive*, making a closer study of the structure of the tree, its various parts, and their functions. They will learn to distinguish the leaves of different trees and study the structure of various types of fruit and their morphological grouping, as well as the action man has taken to develop cultivated varieties of fruit trees, the contributions of individuals and even of anonymous tribes in the past to the process of developing cultivated fruit trees, and the role of citrus fruit in the economy of Israel. Here the children are given the possibility to learn according to different levels of interest. One group will investigate the working conditions of seasonal workers (who pick fruit in Israel) and compare these with the conditions of workers at the regional packing plant that is run jointly by the kibbutzim in the region. A second group will undertake a special assignment—growing a specimen of Mediterranean fruit fly and observing its development—while others will do the same with other types of fruit pests and study the methods of combating pests. Still another group will study how the fruit from our orange groves reaches the tables of private homes in other countries.

The individual work assigned to the children in connection with the project corresponds to their level of knowledge and is divided into various stages of study. Here is an example of a set of instructions.

Citrus Groves in Our Country

1. In the book *The Citrus Grove* you will find a list of the places where citrus fruits are cultivated, as well as statistics regarding the distribution of citrus groves in the country.
    a. Copy the list in neat writing, and write out the figures in words.
    b. Locate the places on the map.
    c. On your map, using different colors, shade in the places where oranges and grapefruit are grown.
2. Which district of Israel has a large number of citrus groves?
3. Refer to the soil distribution map, and prepare for the final discussion on the subject. In what month does the orange-picking season begin in the Jezreel Valley, and when does it begin in the Coastal Plain?
4. Note the region of the country where grapefruit grows most

plentifully and where oranges take second place, noting all the varieties grown.

From the charts accompanying the citrus grove project, the children learn how to read numbers greater than 1,000 and how to read maps. They become aware of the connection between economics, the climatic and geographical conditions of the country, and sources of livelihood. The problem confronting the teaching staff of Kibbutz Artzi is how to bridge the gap between the subject matter—which is in the nature of one layer upon another (in terms of the level of difficulty and the inner logic)—and the project as a totality.

We have already mentioned that the method adopted was to work out a program of projects in which gradation in the teaching of theoretical subjects and manual skills would be preserved and where the necessary level of practice exercises and review would also be provided, without affecting the integrity and vitality of the projects themselves. This is a delicate and complex task, requiring close adherence to principle and sincerity, as well as recognition of the limitations of the method. If a certain subject or manual skill does not fit in organically with a certain project—i.e., if it does not contribute to the children's understanding of the subject or expand their field of interest, if it does not illuminate a specific aspect of the project as a life-unit, or if it does not emanate from it—then no attempt is made to transplant it into the project artificially. Instead, it is studied separately, outside its framework, as we shall explain below.

Botany, zoology, the history of civilization, the geography and history of Israel, citizenship, and agriculture are subjects that are an integral part of life for the kibbutz child, and they are at the focus of many of the projects. These topics have been planned and balanced in the annual curriculum of every class, as we have pointed out, and the principle of gradation is also carefully preserved. Following is an explanation of how the study of the history and geography of Israel is graded for different levels, and how reviewing is accomplished:

In the third grade, in the projects "From One Morning to the Next" and "The River," the pupils learn about the *winds* and the *compass*. In the fourth grade, in the projects "Our Kibbutz," "The Citrus Grove," and "The Home," there is a review of these subjects; in addition, the children learn to read a *chart* and a *map*.

In the fifth grade, they study the *map of Israel* in connection with the project dealing with the region in which the children's home village is situated. The same year, in the project "Explorers of the World," they learn about the *globe* and the *world map*.

In the sixth year, under the subject of "Haifa and its Environs" (as well as in "The Middle East" and "General Geography"), they revise and extend in depth their study of "The Map of Israel and Its Regions."

Following is an example from the program of natural sciences:

In the third grade, in connection with the project "The Tree," the children study the main parts of the plant: the root, the trunk, and the leaves. In the fourth grade, for "The Citrus Groves," the subject is studied in greater depth, with concepts of conditions for growth and a detailed study of varieties of fruit. During the fifth grade study of the project "The Bee and the Flower," the structure of the flower is investigated. In the sixth grade, for the project "Field and Garden," there is a review of all the parts of the plant, but at a higher level of understanding: seeds, germination, and plant nutrition.

Review (or revision) is correctly considered one of the *conditions for learning*, since it is the means of ensuring that the pupil remembers the material and that it becomes a vital part of his own store or knowledge. However, review by no means implies *mechanical repetition*. Educational research has led to the conclusion that the most effective method of review is that which presents previously learned material in a new combination. Under the project system, the content learned comes up anew in different contexts and in varied combinations. For example, the world map is studied in the context of the projects "Explorers of the World"; "Fire" in the context of petroleum resources; "The Field and the Garden" in the context of the origin of various fruit and vegetables; and "Haifa and Its Environs" in connection with the question of where the ships that call at Haifa port came from.

However, the main value of this program of learning, with familiar subjects coming up in new combinations, is that it *trains the child to transfer the knowledge he has acquired from one sphere to another, promotes the process of forming generalizations, and helps him to understand the connection between things.* And herein lies the fundamental objective of teaching.

We have seen that the integration of academic subjects in the project enriches and deepens the learning process. We have described the subjects that can be organically integrated within the projects studied. Now let us consider the difficulties that arise in coordinating the teaching of the Hebrew language and of arithmetic, subjects which can only rarely be placed at the center of activity when working on a project but which must be taught consecutively throughout the year, with systematic grading of study material and review.

Language Teaching in the Project Method

The teaching of the native language is justifiably considered to be one of the primary functions of the school. Proper knowledge of the language helps in a clearer comprehension of the environment, in an accurate understanding of concepts and terms, and in developing the ability to formulate ideas and express them succinctly.

Without language there can be no communication; it is a medium of creativity. In the social context, language is the setting of the national culture, and adequate language instruction is particularly important in a country whose population is largely composed of immigrants.

Research into the methods of learning the language has shown that formal teaching via the traditional "Hebrew lesson" does not yield satisfactory results; knowledge of the rules of grammar does not improve a child's language. Language study must be functional: the child must learn it through its usage in everyday life in his general school activity. Written composition, too, should emanate from plenty and not from dearth; in other words, it should be a matter of the child's expressing himself because of an inner need to communicate something. In the schools where "composition" is taught as an exercise for its own sake, and not as a means of expressing something in context, the child learns to write by using routine formulas—"what the teacher expects us to write"—but this does not help him achieve what every cultured person badly needs: the ability to organize and express feelings and thoughts.

The children write out of a need to speak, to define, to describe, to relate, and to sum up. However, even though the motivation for self-expression is inherent in the project method and there is ample opportunity for verbal and written expression by the children, this in itself is no guarantee that they will acquire correct knowledge of the language. It is in this fertile soil that deliberate, planned language instruction must be sown. How is this done? The teacher draws on the linguistic material in the project units. Every day a talk is held in class for the purpose of improving the use of the language, ingraining the means of expression, and enriching the vocabulary. In the fourth to sixth grades, grammar rules and formations are studied.

Instruction, it has been shown, is continuous. It may also be asked if it is planned. Some pedagogues are opposed to any planning in language instruction, maintaining that there is no better way to learn the language than through teaching "when the occasion arises," i.e., when a child comes across the need to use a certain expression or stumbles upon a language problem. The seeds of learning sown in this manner doubtless fall on fertile soil and yield a good harvest, but one can hardly rely on teaching "as the opportunity arises" for complete language instruction. Under the project method, our teachers try to *help the opportunites to arise* through deliberate planning.

The Teaching of Mathematics in the Project Method

Important objectives in mathematics teaching can be attained with the project method: the children learn to think in terms of quantities, and they acquire a mathematical approach to the world, an understanding of the social value of mathematics, and a mastery of the methods of solving practical problems. The project raises questions that call for a mathematical solution: the economic viability of a given branch in the kibbutz economy; balancing the economy; surveying; the distance between settlements; the speed of vehicles and of animals; crop yields; population density; dates; etc.

Such vital questions, when tackled by the children in the course of work on a specific project, are far removed from the kind of "problems" posed in the conventional arithmetic textbook, where the child must force himself to work while his mind is occupied with questions of an entirely different nature. But study within the context of the project is unlikely to achieve the necessary thorough grounding in mathematics, for the project's elements in themselves are not sufficient to turn the child's knowledge of mathematics into a practical tool. It is therefore necessary to conduct concentrated mathematical exercises, followed by periodic review. Furthermore, instruction in mathematics requires very careful grading, and we must ask whether it is possible to coordinate this with the project method.

Recent staff discussions at Kibbutz Artzi have dealt with new ways of teaching mathematics in the light of revolutionary methods changes introduced over the past decade. The following conclusions on mathematics teaching and the project method were reached: Insofar as the project involved a mathematical aspect, the teaching of mathematics should be conducted in the context of the project. If, however, there is no such aspect in the project, it is advisable to undertake special minor mathematical projects—e.g., measuring instruments, the kibbutz in statistics; our winter clothing; the cost of a trip; the budget for upkeep of a child and an adult in the kibbutz; etc. Proper grading is ensured through a collection of mathematical problems adapted to various projects and supplied as an aid to the teacher.

Mathematics is taught, in part, outside the context of the project, by the graded method. However, even this does not involve a formal, conventional method which relies solely on books. Variety is ensured by (1) short projects "arising according to opportunity"; (2) special classroom corners for mathematical activity, with measuring, weighing, and calculating instruments; (3) individual and group mathematical games for practice and exercise purposes; (4) pages of exercises, which do not have to be copied out; and (5) the textbook, which thus becomes *one* of the learning aids, and not the main or sole object around which teaching takes place.

Here is an example of how mathematics is fitted into a project in the fourth grade:

From this page you will learn the distances between the varieties of trees in the orange grove, and whether the soil is properly utilized.

1. Begin work only after reading all the instructions carefully.
2. Assemble your materials: tape measure, pencil, notebook, and rope. Now go to the orange grove with your partner and do the following:
   a. Measure the distance between the trees in the lemon, grapefruit, orange, and tangerine sections, noting the results in your notebook.
   b. Measure the circumferences of the trunks of different varieties of fruit trees (two of each kind), and note your results.
   c. Estimate the circumference of the foliage of the varieties of fruit trees.
   d. Work out a method to verify your estimate (remember the methods you have used in the past). Write down your answer.
3. Answer the following questions:
   a. Are all the different kinds of trees equal in circumference?

    b. If their circumferences are not equal, give the reason.

    c. Explain why such large distances have been left between the trees. Isn't it a pity to waste so much ground?

    d. Compare the circumference of the foliage of the trees in the orange grove, and estimate the area taken up by the roots. (Write down your estimates—you will find the right answer later.)

    e. Is a tall tree better than a short one? Give the reasons for your view.

    f. Does the farmer "interfere" with the way the tree grows: If so, how?

Teaching Outside the Framework of the Project Method

Does the project method claim to encompass all of the child's learning at school? Certainly not. Children of seven to twelve offer very fertile soil for teaching and for absorbing a myriad of impressions, and every possible means of conveying knowledge to them must be exploited—many gates to the acquisition of knowledge must be opened.

The kibbutz school has evolved the following ways of influencing this objective: *the book corner*, with guidance for general reading; *the newspaper corner* and *discussions* on events in Israel and on the international scene; *social gatherings*, with programs devoted to a personality, an event, or a radio or musical program; and *meetings* with parents, other kibbutz members, and guests. All of these are educational-social activities of a kind that, in the state schools, come under the category of "supplementary education." Apart from this, there is also regular teaching, throughout the school year, of certain areas of schooling not covered by the project method.

Since the kibbutz school places strong emphasis on "supplementary education," which is included in the framework of general schooling, it is worth mentioning here the forms it assumes in the elementary school:

1. *Physical education*, including calisthenics, sports, rhythmics, and dance. The last two generally play some part in most of the projects on which young children work.

2. *Music*, including singing, learning to read music, recorder playing, music appreciation, and the history of music. Singing and the playing of instruments are part of every project, particularly for the younger age groups. However, musical education is also to a large extent conducted outside the framework of the project.

3. *English* (the first foreign language)—teaching is begun in the fifth grade.

4. *Weekly nature walks* foster an emotional attachment to the surroundings. They are a practical way of becoming acquainted with nature, and teach children to observe the cycles of animal and plant life and of the elements.

One day in the week is set aside for the nature walk. (In the sixth grade, because of the full curriculum, the schedule is only once every two weeks.) The study program is worked out to correspond to the seasons and to the age of the children. The walk concludes with a discussion, a small exhibition, or some written work.

If, in every grade, projects are undertaken which center around themes of nature, and if excursions form part of the program of learning, it may be asked why these extra "nature walks" are necessary. The answer is that these weekly and year-round walks bring home to the children the unity of the cycle of growth and the influence of the seasons on all natural phenomena, and instill in them an awareness of, and a feeling for, these phenomena.

5. *Walks around the kibbutz farm.* At first glance, it may seem paradoxical to suggest that kibbutz children have to be taken around the farm of their own kibbutz. One might well imagine that they are quite familiar with various sections of the farm and with regular and seasonal work cycles. However, we must draw a distinction here between familiarity with outward appearances and deliberate study of what is actually taking place around the farm and in the other kibbutz work areas. When accompanied by their teacher, the children pose questions, and a causative approach is fostered which develops their ability to think independently about farm processes and to understand them.

Over the years, as the kibbutzim have grown in size and prospered, there has been a tendency to build the residential quarters at a considerable distance from the farm section (in the past the entire kibbutz area was usually smaller). This has made it necessary to seek deliberate ways of keeping the children aware of farm processes, instilling in them a knowledge and an understanding of the various branches of the kibbutz economy—not only of the farm but also of the workshops and service branches. In the course of projects, they learn about certain aspects of the kibbutz economy (for example, "The Citrus Grove," "The Olive Grove," "Wood," "The Land of Israel," and "Our Kibbutz").

The tours around the kibbutz are aimed at making the children familiar with those processes in the kibbutz economy which are not likely to serve as a specific source of study material in the elementary school grades, or which cannot be included in the study program because of lack of time (agricultural machinery and tools, the irrigation system, crop rotation, livestock branches, workshops, services, etc.). Although these tours do not involve thorough and detailed study, they expand the children's understanding of the economic organization of the society in which they live, and of its achievements, and they heighten an appreciation of the difficulties that must be overcome. They also provide a practical basis for theoretical studies in the years to come.

The visit to the kibbutz farm section is scheduled for the first study period one day every two weeks. It is planned in advance. The children meet the director and the staff of the particular farm or service branch they are visiting, they pose questions, and they listen to explanations of work processes, profitability, specific difficulties, etc. Every tour is summarized by one of the children in a "Notebook on the Kibbutz Economy" or in the group's journal.

6. *Weekly discussions on Israel and world news.* A regular day and time are set aside for these discussions, the subjects of which are determined in advance. The children prepare for the event by reading up on the topic in the press and by discussing it with their parents and other adults.

7. *Guidance in general reading.* The teacher-counselor takes an interest in the general reading of all the children in his charge, guiding each one individually. Apart from this personal guidance, a weekly group discussion is held on books read by the children. One of the pupils relates the subject of a book he had read, or the group discusses something they have all read. They compare evaluations of types of books and approaches to reading, and recommend interesting books to each other.

Literature is studied mainly as an integral part of the project, for there are human, emotional, artistic, and philosophical aspects to every project. However, it is not always possible to find stories or poems of literary value to go with every project; when this is the case, literature is taught outside the framework of the project. In the fifth and sixth grades this is a deliberate policy because it is felt that children of ten or eleven should be taught to appreciate literature for its own sake, without any connection with the subject being studied in class.

8. *Social gatherings devoted to personalities and events.* These affairs have a double purpose: they are an educational factor in helping to mold the social group, and they are a way of teaching children about the history of the Jewish people, Zionism, and the State of Israel. Although these topics are touched on in many of the projects, they cannot be as fully covered as their importance requires.

9. *The annual excursion.* Every year the group sets out on an excursion of several days to a particular part of the country. In the fifth and sixth grades, this trip is part of the project dealing with a certain region. For example, schools in the north study the "Jezreel Valley" in the fifth grade, while schools in the south study "The Judean Hills." In the sixth grade, in connection with "The City" project, the children visit Tel Aviv, Haifa, or Jerusalem and the surrounding district of that city.

In the third and fourth grades, the annual excursion is not linked with any project. Its purpose is to gain general impressions of the landscape of the country, to be exposed to different ways of life and, above all, to serve as a major social event in the life of the group.

We have described in some detail certain fundamental aspects of the project method, a method of education and teaching based on the interest, the needs, and the active participation of the child, a method that imparts knowledge and skills and develops the faculty of thinking while at the same time instilling values. The project method has achieved these goals by abolishing the conventional division of study into separate subjects and by drawing up a curriculum of life-units in which the child learns concepts and acquires knowledge. This is not easy, as we see in observing the efforts required of teacher-counselors in endeavoring to preserve the complex combination of specific subjects of study within the project as an integral whole.

Our educators, however, have taken this difficult and complex path in order to ensure that learning is derived from natural motivations—the desire for knowledge, curiosity, and the urge for discovery and activity. They do not seek to satisfy this desire on the spot but, rather, to stimulate the aspiration for achievement, which implies a readiness to forego immediate satisfactions for the sake of a greater purpose. However, teachers in the kibbutz schools also base their education and teaching on additional motives in the child's personality, motive forces that constitute a basis for learning and for the child's personal and social development.

The Group and the Teacher-Counselor

It is well known that seven- to twelve-year-olds have a strong need to belong to a group. They derive a sense of security from this feeling of belonging, just as, at a younger age, the feeling of attachment to their parents once imbued them with a sense of confidence. It is a vital requirement of the child to feel that he is a needed member of a group, that he works for it and is an active participant in it, or even that he merely belongs to it and has a place within it. The child proudly shares the attitudes and values of his group. There is no doubt that the ability to influence these attitudes and values is a powerful educational spring-board. How can the group counselor acquire such influence, and how can he divert this group energy to worthwhile social-educational aims?

The educational project, by its very nature, is a fitting objective for joint activity by this age group. Is there a group of children anywhere who would not naturally be attracted to a challenge, to the investigation inherent in the project, and to the lively activity required and the many different jobs to be undertaken by independent teams? The project itself, however, is only a means; its influence depends principally upon the way it is handled by the teacher-counselor. How does the counselor educate his group?

The child treasures his group, as does the educator. The children are deeply concerned about the prestige of their group, and they preserve its unity at all costs. Herein lies a powerful educational force, which the teacher must respect and know how to channel. He respects their inde-pendence, stimulates them to initiative, and at the same time preserves his own leadership. Based on his knowledge, experience, and personality, the children regard him as an authority. To them, he represents the society in which their parents live and with which they identify. Just and correct behavior on his part, and a friendly attitude toward the children, will turn him into a genuine authority in their eyes. He does not have to act "authoritatively" to acquire his status. Instead of assuming the initiative himself, he influences his pupils to do so; instead of getting things done himself, he stimulates them to activity; and instead of pro-viding easy answers to questions, he points the way for them to find their own answers, arousing their thought processes. His authority is not assured merely because of his status as a teacher—it is something he must build up through his personality, behavior, and attitudes.

Under the guidance of the teacher-counselor, study of the project becomes the objective of the group. Is there any child who will not be ready to put all he has into achieving a goal that is highly evaluated by his own group?

Most children join in with the group that is engaged in the project. However, most groups have a few children who are different—individuals who, for some reason, do not have any feeling of belonging to the group. They keep away from it, disappointed, despairing, and indifferent, or embittered and aggressive. In some cases this is due to a deep disturbance in the personality of the child, and psychological treatment is required.

In the majority of cases, however, the teacher-counselor is capable of helping the child to find his place in the group and thereby stimulate him to learn. What we have here would seem to be a vicious cycle. The child does not participate in the work of the group *because* he does not feel that he belongs to it. And the fact that the child does not participate or contribute to the activities of the group is a factor in his feeling of not belonging. This vicious cycle has to be broken down by the teacher-counselor. How?

Under the project method, he has the possibility of discovering the particular aptitudes of every child, "the ability to do something special." For example, in the project "Discoverers of the World," some children set out to investigate trade routes at the time of the discoveries. Some draw maps; others list categories of agricultural produce according to climatic regions; and still others make small drawings of the products on the map itself, to indicate where they are produced. Some build models of ships of bygone ages; others construct a relief map in the sand; some select pictures to illustrate the theme; others are busy rehearsing a play, a song, dances, etc.

In the school which confines itself to theoretical work, the group holds in esteem only the intellectual child, and the child whose aptitudes are more of a practical nature will feel unable to contribute. This is not the case with the project, where aptitudes in both the theoretical and the practical fields are required. With the help of the teacher-counselor, almost every child can find a field of activity in which he can give of his abilities to the group and even prove to be outstanding in a particular sphere. In this way he becomes one of the group and feels that its aims are his own. The teacher-counselor knows the group as a whole and its collective needs, but at the same time he gives individual attention to each child—he is concerned that each child participate in the life of the group and come under its educational influence.

This is how the project method constructs its method of education and teaching on the basis of a key motivating factor—the desire to belong.

The Desire for Achievement
Rather than Competition for Grades

The ambition to achieve is as important a motive for activity by the child as it is for the adult. Delight at the discovery of skill is one of the greatest sources of happiness in life, and the aspiration for this is one of the most cogent stimuli to action. While this motive is a vital factor in education and learning, its influence is positive only if the child regards positive aims as achievements.

We have already discussed the child's identification with the values of his group and its educator, and have pointed out that the educator-counselor guides the group toward learning and educational achievements and helps each child to find a place in the group and make his contribution within it. We have spoken of the project method, which offers many ways of learning and contributes to the child's feeling of achievement. Practice continually reconfirms the fact that if a child's ability in any field of manual skill, physical fitness, or artistic aptitude is accorded recognition, he will make rapid progress in areas of theoretical study in which he previously encountered considerable difficulties.

Are there other ways of stimulating each child to individual learning?

The ambition to achieve has always been identified with the desire to outdo others in competition. It was the conventional view that children should be given incentives to better learning: good marks and prizes for success and punishment for failure. But competition in learning undermines the personal and social values of those who do well: they develop characteristics of exaggerated self-confidence, feelings of superiority, and the desire to outshine others rather than a striving for knowledge itself. As for those who lose out in the race, their failure, measured against the achievements of those who excel, is exaggerated beyond all proportion, and their actual achievements are belittled to less than their true abilities. Learning for the sake of good marks tends to put a damper on initiative, on in-depth study, and on true creativity, while it stimulates speed and quantity rather than profound invididual thought and a concern for quality.

Progressive schools are very careful in selecting methods to stimulate learning, since the mental health of the pupil and the group spirit of the class depend on them. These schools prefer to set realistic goals for each pupil—goals toward which he is capable of advancing—rather than have him compete with his colleagues, continually comparing his achievements with theirs.

The teacher-counselor in the kibbutz school encourages his pupils to advance within the limits of their abilities. He motivates the learning of each child by formulating short-range objectives for him, objectives that are not easily attainable without effort but are by no means beyond the child's reach.

What the teacher expects differs for each child, and the child shares the teacher's expectations; together they decide on the goals and evaluate the pupil's progress. Every step taken toward mobilizing all the child's forces is something of a "success," for the measure of success is the progress made by the child rather than the result of his efforts in comparison with a certain objective which the whole class was supposed to reach. And along with success comes self-confidence, accompanied by the striving for further achievements.

Is the sole purpose of this method to set attainable goals for every child and to encourage him to share his teacher's expectations and evaluation? Anyone familiar with school life knows how encouraging this method is, how much it strenghtens the striving for achievement among the vast majority of children—all the "average" children who will never, with the greatest effort in the world, achieve the highest marks—and how it opens up the path for the free development of the forces latent in "talented" children whose progress is generally held back by the expectation of "a certain achievement" from "the entire class."

It is sometimes asked whether our schools do not make good use of the competitive spirit that is so strong in childhood. The kibbutz school does practice competition in various fields, with one group competing against another of the same level. Such competitions have all the excitement of the competitive fight for victory, but they also educate the children in the spirit of group unity and responsibility.

This view of competition in education is identical with the general kibbutz concept of the individual who works according to his ability and develops his gifts in order to build both his own personality and his group. In considering the attitude to personal education inherent in this philosophy, the following extract from an ancient prayer conveys its essence:

> Give us the *peace of mind to accept* those things which cannot be changed, the courage to *change* those which it is within our *power* to change, and the *wisdom* to differentiate between the two.

In this survey we have reviewed the educational and teaching features of the project method, which is geared to the child's inner motivation, his curiosity, the desire to belong to a group, and the ambition for achievement. Since psychology regards these motivations as fundamental to the psyche of the child, a method based upon them has deep roots.

What remains for us now is to consider in greater detail the personal and social attitudes and views which the school advocates in its education with respect to the content and methods of teaching.

The Means and Goals of Education

It is generally agreed that the general values and outlook of society and its educational goals are identical. But there is as yet little evidence, in practice, of that obvious educational truth—namely, that in order for that education to be fully realized, there must be harmony between the *goal* and the *means* of education.

At the present time we find a muddle of progressive educational goals, deriving from a democratic society and coexisting with outdated educational means that are suited to educational aims based on the philosophy of past centuries.

Obedience to authority is an educational goal based on a philosophical outlook that is diametrically opposed to the goal of developing in the child the powers of self-control and discipline, the ability to take independent decisions, and the qualities of respect and consideration for others.

Progressive educational goals are affirmed the world over: education toward freedom, democracy, and the capacity for team work. But the means employed have not changed, and in most schools the basis of authoritarianism in education still prevails. Can these goals be achieved if the means are not compatible with them?

In the kibbutz school the child is educated to love knowledge, to be independent, to feel an obligation to society, to aspire for achievements that are compatible with the values of the society in which he lives, to be considerate to his fellow man and his individuality, and to appreciate and be capable of team work. In our review of the project method we have attempted to illustrate the degree to which the educational means employed in this method are identical with the aims—an identity that is key to the educational process.

Conclusion

The project method is compatible with kibbutz society and expresses its values. But as a highly recommended form of progressive education, it can also be applied in any other kind of society and way of life.

The advantage of the kibbutz school is that it is anchored in a society which does not pay mere lip service to the values it affirms, but attempts to fulfill them despite difficulties and occasional stormy clashes between the old and the new. In kibbutz education, not only are the educational means identical with the values of the society, but the education is identical with the society itself—as it were, an education within education and a society within a society. And that is a rare thing indeed.

a way to integrate kibbutz values with personal yearnings

The Youth Society

by Moni Alon

There is a great difference between the atmosphere in a young children's society of 50 to 60 children and a high school youth society with 150 to 200 members. Conditions in the latter afford opportunities for much more social contact: the children meet in the dining room, on the sport grounds, during recess games, at parties and cultural activities, in discussions organized by the youth society, and at hikes and other joint projects. The youth society resembles a federation of educational groups who live and learn together; each group is autonomous but cooperates with the others in arranging social and cultural activities.

All affairs within the youth society are handled by committees, whose members are elected by various educational groups. With representatives of the older group (16 to 18 years of age) acting as leaders, the committees organize cultural activities, sport programs, and the landscaping of the school area; they issue a newspaper, supervise discussions, and see

97

to it that decent relations are maintained among the children and between the educational groups. In cases of conflict or a breach of discipline, the appropriate committee arranges for a hearing. Staff representatives (teachers and metaplot) advise and help to coordinate these
activities with the general plans of the school.

Once in a while the entire youth society meets in assembly to discuss
such issues as the absorption of city children; discipline and study; plans
for hikes or for visits to settlements with a different social structure; a
mock trial on social or political events; literature sessions; etc. All the
children participate in the assembly to vote and adopt resolutions that
speak in the name of the youth society as a whole.

Questions of health, budget, security, and curriculum do not fall
under the jurisdiction of the youth society. There is a growing tendency,
however, for each year's graduating class to assume responsibility for the
society for the next year. The graduates submit an annual plan for an
overall social mission, for organizational or technical changes to raise the
level of efficiency, etc.

The youth society's autonomy depends on several factors: the participation of the society as a whole, the guiding role of the graduating
class, and the advice of adult representatives (this advice is not always
accepted, and the adolescents then learn from their own mistakes).

The educational influence of the youth society is important in that it
complements that of the educational group. The group represents a
permanent and orderly home, with stable relations and well-defined
demands on each student's social behavior, but the youth society provides an arena for the more dynamic activity of the adolescent. (Children
in elementary school do not require this more extensive framework for
play, friendly discussion, and a social milieu.) In high school we see the
gradual transition from life in an intimate educational group to participation in the activity of a broader youth society.

The desire for contacts outside the educational group, so typical
among youngsters of 15 to 16 and older, is met by the broader high
school setting. Here they can find outlets for their initiative, for showing
off, even for aggressive drives, all of which can be partly channeled into
creative and socially conscious directions.

The activities of the youth society, the desire of individuals to excel,
and the efforts by the educational group to "maintain its good standing"—all these are important outlets for a high level of energy. The
extracurricular and self-directed programs include sports, planning and
executing holiday celebrations, participating in a choir or orchestra,
playing a musical instrument, dancing, and other hobbies—activity that

balances out the strictly defined duties imposed by the school and the social structure.

Mozart Week (Reported by Yaacov Dror, Kibbutz Dalia)

The initiative came from the children. Preparations lasted for months, and the teachers cooperated. The choir and orchestra were busy for many weeks.

"Mozart Week" (in the high school of Harei Efraim) opened with an instructive lecture by M. Ravina, who gave a picture of Mozart's personality and surveyed the main periods in the composer's creative life.

The second evening featured a concert by the high school students. Interspersed with the musical program were readings from letters by Mozart. The high school choir of 100 and a string orchestra participated, as did various chamber music groups. The evening ended with audience participation in singing well-known Mozart songs.

The third evening was a record concert of Mozart's "Requiem." A pamphlet was distributed, containing a Hebrew translation of the Latin text, with an explanation of the musical structure of the work and illustrations for the musical score. The evening made a lasting impression on the young audience.

On the final evening a fifty-piece orchestra played "Serenade for Strings." Chamber groups and vocalists performed. The evening was most enjoyable for participants and audience alike. In addition, all music lessons that week were devoted to Mozart's work for varied instruments and ensembles.

Much effort was put into this project, and the participants were pleased. Perhaps the most satisfying was the feeling that this was not a project by individuals, but a joint effort of the youth society as a whole. This was what guaranteed its success and its educational value.

In planning its cultural life, the youth society fosters active participation, thereby attempting to offset the effects of the passive entertainment offered by the mass media. In this respect, it is the carrier of a particular kind of socialization.

To a large extent, kibbutz education uses the "secret ingredient of success"—the fact that a young adolescent is much more deeply affected by an older peer than by an adult teacher. The youngster is naturally drawn to a person close to his own age, who becomes a model for identification and self-education; the sublimated unconscious drives that exist between members of the same sex at this age can turn naturally into heterosexual friendships, under the unspoken guidance of older students. In addition, the influence of these older students minimizes any tendencies toward mischief by the younger children and their groups. Thanks to the many-faceted activities of the youth society, our educational institutions have become much more than high schools. We believe that the student's deep emotional identification with his school derives from the independent programs and autonomy of the youth society.

Of course, this intensive life is not without problems, one of which affects mainly the older students: the heavy load of work and activity. A considerable number of students—especially the more active ones—complain about insufficient time to pursue their interest in some subjects. (When our graduates go to the Army, they begin to criticize various aspects of their high school experience; as a result of some of their criticism, student work assignments have been reduced from 15 to 12 hours weekly in the last year of high school.) However, despite these understandable reactions, the youth society is the major factor in the personal and social structure of their maturation.

Changes in the Educational Group During Adolescence

Changes in the educational group during the high school years are related to the school's educational goals and to its social-psychological character. When the school is a joint enterprise of several kibbutzim, the student body is enlarged and the educational groups are changed. This gives us an opportunity to improve the social standing of those children who may have experienced some difficulty in their elementary school groups. Moreover, meeting children from other kibbutzim is a novel social experience. The educational group is frequently expanded from 15 or 18 children to about 22 or 25 (the increase is usually due to the absorption of several city children).

Basically, the educational group continues to carry out its function of socialization and mutual aid, but it now plays a more important role as the framework for social relations, activity, and play. The desire for increased emotional distance from one's parents sets in, and there is a general insecurity vis-à-vis the demands of the adult world. Behavior norms are crystallized and become more conscious and well defined; public opinion is a weightier factor, as are the internal "institutions"—the group committee and the group discussions.

In a school that does not employ coercion or punishment, public opinion is of great value: it leads to inner identification with behavior patterns that are democratically decided upon. Public opinion is also effective in interpersonal relations and in evaluating the subjective efforts invested by the child in his studies, even if the objective achievements vary in accordance with different abilities. Class composition is not based on the principle of homogeneous ability because a mixed setting, in our opinion, creates a healthier educational climate.

The autonomy of the group increases. A committee elected by the group for a half-year period is responsible for clipping newspapers and suggesting reading material. The committee also makes recommendations about financial expenditures and objects of joint ownership; it arranges for hearings to settle conflicts among group members or complaints about classroom misbehavior. The autonomy of the group is not absolute, however; committee meetings and hearings are attended by the teacher-educator and the metapelet.

Group problems are discussed at weekly group meetings, as are theoretical and general subjects (social and political current events).

Literary "trials" are conducted both in the educational group and in the youth society. The educator and his group select a story in which a personal, moral, or social problem is involved. Members of the group assume the roles of the prosecutor, the defense, judges, and witnesses. The trial attempts to cover every aspect of the problem, and by dramatizing the various roles the children identify with the characters of the story and with their problems. The preparation sometimes lasts several weeks, and the trial becomes a serious joint project for the group, concentrating the interest and activity of the members.

A Literary Trial (Reported by Yehudith Hazan, Kibbutz Mishmar Ha'emek)

When I first began to work with ninth graders (age 15), I noticed several major educational problems: the boys in my group were dominant numerically (3:2) as well as in influence. There was much tension in interpersonal relations. Many of the boys were highly intelligent, but completely uninterested in social studies, and they lacked any urge to overcome intellectual obstacles. In contrast, they were very active in sports. I came to the conclusion that it would be advisable to arrange a literary trial whose subject matter, while of intellectual interest, would afford an outlet for their competitive drives.

We selected a story by Herzl, "Solon in Lydia" (this fitted in with the historical period we were dealing with in the class-room). We read the story. The group committee elected members for the various roles: three for the prosecution and three for the defense, and two students and the teacher-counselor served as judges. Other members of the group were requested to be witnesses for the prosecution or the defense.

The story is placed in Lydia, 585 B.C. A young Greek, Enkosmos, asks to marry the daughter of King Barzus and promises, in return, to deliver to the king and his people an invention: a machine which produces, with no work input, unlimited amounts of flour for all the people. At that time Solon was visiting Lydia; when Solon heard about the invention, he advised the king to destroy it and put the inventor to death. The prosecution charged Enkosmos with being guilty, while the defense tried to justify him. After the defense and prosecution had completed the investigation of their respective witnesses, they presented their concluding speeches. The final verdict was decided upon by the entire group, who voted on two issues: (1) Was Enkosmos guilty? The majority decided that the blame should not fall on him personally, but rather on the rulers of Lydia who accepted the invention and made bad use of it. (2) Was it a positive invention for those times? The majority agreed that the society at that time was not yet able to benefit from such an invention.

The trial contributed to the consolidation of the group. The members derived much satisfaction from the intellectual give-and-take, which, despite some momentary friction between the two sides, raised the level of the group and increased its interest in societal problems.

Life in the group is not always smooth and reassuring; there are feuds, jealousies, and sometimes even hidden struggles for power. However, with time, as the children learn to recognize the weak and strong points of their peers, they try to avoid clashes with them.

In the 12-to-14 age group, children often behave like a "herd," spending most of their free time together and demanding of one another solidarity and, to some extent, excessive conformity. In the higher grades this tendency is weakened in favor of differentiation of interests and respect for individual inclinations. One of the tasks of the educator is to help establish an atmosphere of tolerance and privacy, and to oppose regressive trends that arise from time to time and exert pressure to return to the herd-like tempo. In recent years an attempt has been made to give the children more privacy: the number of individuals sharing a room has been reduced from four to three, and "quiet corners" have been designated in some study rooms. Even though we have not yet found a fully satisfactory solution to this problem, we wish to emphasize that we consider the children's longing for greater privacy and individualization a positive step toward adulthood.

The Role of Teacher-Counselors

The factor that lends our educational framework its unique character is the cultivation of independence, initiative, and autonomy in adolescents. This can be attained by providing wide scope for activities and by establishing challenges to the individual's abilities and to his sense of responsibility. However, this does not mean doing away with the adult's role as guide and instructor. He will be successful in this role only to the degree that he can arouse feelings of identification and closeness in the pupil rather than negative, rebellious feelings (which inevitably result when someone exercises purely formal authority).

The educational authority required of the kibbutz adult during his encounters with pupils should, in the words of Erich Fromm, be "rational and encourage development" rather than rest on formal authority. It should be based on the educator's academic competence, on his ability to instill in his pupils the wish to further their knowledge and their understanding of life, and on a mutual affection after a long period of personal contact.

Anyone who works with young people when their reactions are sometimes spontaneous, instinctive, and to no small extent determined by the pleasure principle, is at one time or another bound to have a passing conflict with one of them. This can be solved either by a personal talk with the individual concerned or by discussing the problem with a group committee.

The stance of the educator vis-à-vis his pupils cannot be purely formal and impersonal, nor can it be dependent purely on the nature of his personal relations. Even though there is little ceremony or formality in the outward relations between adults and pupils, we do not fully negate the distance that should be kept between the adult and the youth (contrary to Neill's view), because to do so would mean to fail to cultivate the inhibitions of culture and the positive manners that are necessary in relations between people everywhere. Furthermore, it would not correspond to the inner anticipations of the young person himself with regard to his relations with adults.

The educator has many opportunities for contact with his group and with individual pupils outside the formal work periods: in the dormitories, in the dining room, and on the school grounds. His principal task is, first and foremost, to stimulate his pupils by posing challenges to them and showing them the way to independent activity and how to cope with excessive group pressure on the individual.

The educator responsible for a group sees to the proper functioning of the school program and conducts weekly group discussions. Apart from this "public" activity, the educator is also expected to know each pupil individually, establish a personal relationship with each one, and still be mindful of his limitations in working with adolescents. Thus, if the youngster feels that the adult respects his views and tendencies and is not forcing his own ideas on him, there is a chance that he will open up.

The educator and the metapelet have a cooperative relationship. The metapelet's knowledge of each child's habits and problems, sometimes the most intimate ones, puts her in the position of being able to help and guide the educator. She tries to impart a warm, homelike atmosphere to the living quarters even when such efforts are treated with considerable indifference by the boys, not to mention occasional displays of deliberate disregard. But an experienced metapelet, through daily work with the youngsters and concern for their everyday needs, can create a personal link with many of those in her charge, particularly the girls.

Thanks to her varied contacts with the young people, the metapelet can supplement the educator's impressions; and together they strive for a more comprehensive understanding of each pupil. They are also responsible for maintaining contacts with the kibbutz of the children in their charge and with their parents; this is done at general parent-teacher meetings and in meetings with individual parents. At the latter, the teachers exchange information on the development, achievements, and problems of a child and learn about his behavior in the family circle.

General educational problems are dealt with (in the form of an educational report) at staff meetings. The kibbutz movement also maintains a child guidance clinic at the Oranim Seminar (see chapters 8 and 9), where problems of the lonely child, learning difficulties requiring special assistance, and other educational questions can be discussed with an advisory committee.

The variety of tasks of the educator in the youth society—in his own group and vis-à-vis his colleagues, and in maintaining links with various kibbutz institutions and with the parents of the children in his charge—

can be a heavy burden. He must also continue his own cultural advancement through serious study and maintain an ever-rising standard of professional work. To ensure the educator's alertness and freshness of approach in his pedagogic work, we try to see to it that, in addition to the fundamental refresher course attended by everyone engaged in this task, he is also granted—once every four or five years—a sabbatical year to work in his own kibbutz. In practice, the form of work and the quality of the relations between the educator and his group vary, depending on the age and character of the group and the individual in it, as well as on the personality of the educator himself. The balance between distance and closeness, and between intervention and nonintervention, required of the educator differs in accordance with the age of the group.

Coeducation and Sex Education

Coeducation plays a major role in the kibbutz educational system. Boys and girls are brought up together in the same groups. They live in the same house from infancy until secondary education, they study and play together, and they are in each other's company during various activities of the youth society. Our aim is to achieve more natural and uninhibited relations between the sexes, free from the severe tension or distorted idealization that sometimes arises as a result of estrangement between the sexes. We strive to educate our children toward greater genuine equality between the sexes and toward mutual consideration and appreciation. The fact that coeducation begins at a tender age does not, of course, rule out the marked trend toward a separation between the sexes in other spheres.

During early adolescence, we see evidence of an increase in tension between the sexes, marked by accusations and teasing. However, fundamentally, even at this stage there is an interaction between the introverted tendency generally characteristic of girls at the stage of puberty and the more extroverted, lively, and noisy tendencies of boys. The girls have the effect of restraining the boys, to some extent, in such matters as rough speech, neglect of personal appearance, and untidiness in their rooms. The lively activity and alertness of the boys militate against the tendency of girls to dwell mainly on personal matters and small talk, and serves to expand their interest in broader topics.

At all stages, the girls participate actively in the management of group affairs, in the youth society, and in the youth movement. We have come to realize that, in the past, this concept of equality between the sexes was sometimes distorted because we put too much emphasis on getting the girls to adapt themselves to qualities that correspond mainly to the needs of boys: the cultivation of motor activity, excellence in sports, and encouragement of puritanical simplicity in outward manners and appearance. Today we are seeking paths that make greater allowances for the specific needs of the adolescent girl, with more consideration for a certain narcissism in respect to outer appearance. However, we try not to make this factor decisive in the evaluation of her entire personality. More attention is paid to differential and voluntary learning of literature, psychology, handicrafts, and rhythmics (all of which are available to both sexes), with the specific aim of meeting the emotional requirements of those girls who are more interested in these subjects. There is a greater measure of separation in sports than in the past. In connection with prevocational training, the girls now have the choice of home economics, education, and child care, in addition to the agricultural and technological trades still open to them.

We are still searching for the golden mean in our approach to the education of girls. We are anxious to educate our girls to grow up as women who find satisfaction in their femininity, in family life, and in the general life of kibbutz society—the future toward which we educate everyone. We hope that they will become individuals who are interested in their work, and we attempt to educate them in such a way that they will want to continue to develop and enrich their lives while working in one sphere of kibbutz life. An education of this kind must necessarily present a realistic picture to the pupils—and to girls in particular—of the problems a kibbutz woman can expect. These problems are undoubtedly more complex than those confronting a man because of the more limited range of professions open to her and the psychological difficulties she has to overcome in gaining a firm foothold in a profession. For this reason it is important to educate our young people, and girls in particular, to realize that even though the kibbutz has solved some major problems in the life of women (such as equality within the family, opportunities for activity in many spheres of kibbutz society, etc.), a considerable number of problems still remain. These will very likely not be solved without a struggle fought out by the next kibbutz generation.

Coeducation at the age of puberty cannot be based solely on the natural links that have existed between boys and girls who have grown up together. This close acquaintance results in a certain de-eroticization between members of the same educational group. Therefore, coeducation is possible only when it forms part of a broader educational setting at various stages of the children's development.

Sex education, as we understand it, should be part and parcel of education in general. But its success depends to a great extent on the overall atmosphere in the secondary school, on the wealth of cultural and social experiences, and on the challenges inherent in the activities that shape the personality.

While we fully realize that these ways to sublimation are essential for building the young person's personality, and that they generally have the effect of limiting the preoccupation with sexual problems, they must not be allowed to sublimate these vital urges altogether. That is why deliberately planned education is necessary in this sphere; it is important to give the young people adequate knowledge of sexual life and help them formulate positive expectations with regard to the future.

We also try to instill in the adolescents the ability and the will to exercise sexual abstinence during the period of their education, a will that is motivated not by inner or external fears but primarily by positive future expectations. Sex education is given in various forms to the adolescents, with the educator taking advantage of spontaneous and coincidental associations. In practice, therefore, sex education is far less schematic than might appear from the following description.

To begin with, sex education is given in the form of scientific and practical information on the physiological aspects of sex life. Pregnancy and birth are partly dealt with in the biological study of "The Human Body." The educator also arranges for a physician to talk with the upper graders about the hygiene of sex life, birth control, and so forth. The young people are also directed to good popular scientific works describing sexual relations. Such instruction is of great importance because it removes the unhealthy atmosphere of sordid secrecy often surrounding the subject. The adolescent should, in the course of time, achieve a more conscious orientation regarding problems of sex, and take an independent, unexaggerated view on the role of sex in his adult life, a view that will be an integral part of his entire concept of life.

The group's talks with the educator and the metapelet include problems presented by the young people themselves, either directly or through an anonymous "question box." Sometimes the educator raises questions which he feels are pertinent to the children at the time. For example, among younger age groups at the secondary school, questions arise concerning relations between boys and girls, attitudes toward masturbation and prostitution, and problems encountered in reading books and newspapers or in seeing films, etc.

At the age of 15 or 16, most girls begin to form relationships with boys in the older groups. We regard the formation of friendly ties as a positive manifestation. Such meetings during adolescence build the personality and are a liberating factor that helps the growing-up process. They help to loosen the infantile emotional attachments of a young person to his parents and to his group, and express a healthy self-confidence on the part of young people with regard to their own sexual identity. Of course, there is still a great deal of egocentricity in these encounters—i.e., the desire to find confirmation of one's own identity in the eyes of a boy or girl friend. In most cases—and we say this with all due caution—even though the personality has not yet reached the point of crystallization at this stage, only when this point is reached can the choice of a partner acquire a genuine individual nature, which will be free of purely incidental sexual attraction.

In our talks with the young people we attempt to portray these relationships as youthful love based on mutual erotic attraction, on the maximum of emotional sincerity that can be attained at this age, on intimate friendship and spiritual partnership, and on self-control on the part of both partners regarding erotic manifestations. From an educational point of view, we do not approve of sexual intercourse between young people during their high school years. The adolescent boy—and even more so the girl, for whom erotic experiences, in the broader sense of the term, are of a more intensive nature—would cross the threshold of this stage of maturity too soon. Such experiences may block their paths to an important source of sublimation which, during the period of schooling, can generally be channeled into studies, into social activity, and into crystallization of the personality. We doubt whether a premature experience would help to cultivate the full sexual identity of the individual (especially of the girl) in the direction of what will later be needed during the stage of adult love and when the family is established (a similar view is expressed by Erikson).

Our educational endeavors are directed no less to opposing any trends to de-eroticization and to sexuality "without illusions" (as is advocated by many contemporary young people and in many films and works of literature). We try, in the kibbutz educational system, to cultivate in our adolescents an erotic expectation of adult love relationships that involve the entire personality of two individuals—the emotional aspect, a spiritual and mental partnership, respect, and especially a sense of responsibility toward one another. But we do not try to force this educational advice on our young people—in the last years of school we emphasize that sexual relations should be the outcome of a personal and responsible decision. We know full well that the individual character of the people involved is much more decisive than any rule, even when we succeed in bridging the gap between the erotic impulse and the realm of personal values and the perspective of personal development.

There are, of course, some young people who follow a different behavior pattern. Nevertheless, based on the evidence of the young people themselves—in conversations and, more significantly, in anonymous questionnaires—the majority of pupils in our secondary schools accept our approach not as something irrational, terrifying, or threatening, but as advice to postpone sexual experience to a later time in order to enable it to be more gratifying.

Explanations and free conversation between the educator and his students may help to curb irrational fears, but they do not eliminate sexual tension and desire. However, in an atmosphere of lively activity rather than boredom, of frequent contact between the sexes (but without artificial eroticism), and of work, sports, and many other emotional outlets, it is doubtful that this inner pressure ever reaches the stage of acute sexual deprivation for most students.

Among the oldest students (17 to 18), the educator attempts to paint a genuine picture, adapted to their level of understanding, regarding the problem of love relations, the family in general and the kibbutz family in particular, and such factors as the compatibility and the maturity required to establish family relationships and to bring children into the world. Here, too, we are engaged in a difficult and not always successful struggle against the growing general trend of lowering the age of marriage and child birth. We realize that the atmosphere that will help to offset this trend cannot be created through education alone, but can be achieved by establishing challenges for activity in the movement as well as opportunities for further studies after the completion of compulsory army service. (It seems that the growing trend among young people to continue their studies, as a step to further integration in the kibbutz, is gradually leading to postponed parenthood, especially in the case of girls.) The value of education is that when the occasion for spontaneous erotic relations arises, the capacity of the youngsters to make a conscious and rational choice is increased.

In summary, we attach the greatest importance to the attempt to give deliberate direction to sex education, an attempt aimed at counteracting the attitudes disseminated by the mass media and the repercussions reaching us of the crisis affecting world youth. It is our purpose to inculcate in our youth a humanist moral criterion which will hopefully be applied even in this intimate sphere.

Ideological Education

Based as it is on ideological foundations, the kibbutz movement attaches great importance to ideological education. Its goal is the education of youth toward a conscious identification with the national and socialist tasks espoused by the movement. In our view, it is impossible to ensure the continuation of the kibbutz way of life in the absence of strong emotional ties to it—love for the kibbutz and for its way of life. But it is also apparent that, within a capitalist environment, it is impossible to maintain attachment to the kibbutz solely on the basis of such motives; it must also stem from ideological firmness. Thus, education must obtain dimensions that are geared to the future—a recognition of the need to attain new achievements, the adaptation of the kibbutz to changing social and technological conditions, and the fulfillment of its ideological mission both within and beyond its framework.

We envisage the education of a personality in which ideology constitutes a vital criterion in its many-faceted inner deliberations and decisions, an ideology which does not accept reality as unchanging and taken for granted, but regards the individual as actively responsible for molding the image and the direction of development of both kibbutz society and society in general. This social aspect of "self-realization"—i.e., the belief in man's commitment to strive to fulfill in his own life the faith he affirms—has been the point of departure of the kibbutz since its inception as a pioneering movement, and to this very day it points the way in our educational work.

In connection with this ideological ideal, the young people who receive their education in the kibbutz have several "natural" advantages as well as certain disadvantages. A more socially oriented personality is the end result of being brought up within the group and the children's society, surrounded by the general atmosphere of kibbutz life. The way of life of the adults and their values concerning work, cooperation, and equality are absorbed by the younger generation in such an atmosphere; in addition, the example of their parents lends these principles an emotional connotation that makes them an integral part of the developing personality. Great importance is also attached to the study projects undertaken by the younger elementary school classes, in the context of which we try to stress humanistic aspects even in the natural sciences. Talks between the educators and their students, and the form in which national festivals are celebrated, are the means of inculcating deeper feelings of solidarity with the Jewish people abroad, a sensitivity to suffering, poverty, and oppression, and an attitude to the Arab nations which preaches fraternity between peoples.

Indeed, Rabin's research (among 10- and 17-year-olds) has shown that the dreams, anxieties, and hidden desires of the children of ten kibbutzim are more "social-oriented" and less egocentric than those of a nonkibbutz control group. Also, a survey of seventy 17-year-olds raised in kibbutzim showed a greater sense of self-criticism and a greater sensitivity to criticism, less of a tendency to discount others, less indifference to their environment, and a greater readiness to act on the basis of conscience than was true for a parallel group of ninety urban young people of the same age.

These socially oriented and altruistic reactions of the young person are the foundation for ideological education in adolescence. Nevertheless, these reactions are not to be confused with the foundation itself, for the main function of ideological education at this age is to transform emotional and sometimes subconscious attitudes into a conscious philosophical set of values. We try in our education to establish a sense of moral values that serves as the basis for a political world outlook. We are not speaking here of views on specific political tactics, but rather of a more fundamental outlook. We do not attempt to supply the children with ready-made answers, but try to instill a sense of commitment toward social problems in general.

This ideological dimension has a considerable impact on many areas of activity in the secondary school—for example, in school studies (particularly in the teaching of social studies and the humanities), great weight is attached to Judaic studies and to the study of Jewish life abroad, to the history of Jewish, Israeli, and general labor movements, and to the social and economic theories which have guided them. It is also evident in the method of teaching history, which is based on a dialectical analysis of historical changes, with special emphasis on contemporary problems. The ideological factor also crops up in the study of general and Hebrew literature, when the human and structural aspects inherent in the work are analyzed together with the more formal literary-esthetic aspects. In the weekly group meetings with the educator, both contemporary issues and general abstract principles are discussed, depending upon the age of the members—the problem of the individual and society, happiness and wealth, technological advance and general progress, equality between men and women, equality between peoples and races, peace and war, etc. These subjects, treated generally when first raised, are progressively dealt with in a more concrete and realistic manner in later school years.

In the eleventh grade (ages 16 to 17), for example, some of the topics brought up at meetings with the educator include:

Israel and the Kibbutz
Immigrant absorption in the country and the kibbutz
Israeli society and the kibbutz within it
Other kibbutz movements
The meaning of "pioneering" today

General Subjects
Censorship in the arts
Censorship of the press
Nuclear disarmament
"Light Program" (a popular radio entertainment program)

Israeli and world political problems are also discussed. But with every age group the purpose is always to cultivate critical and principled thinking concerning events and problems that go beyond natural, spontaneous, and egocentric reactions. In these talks, especially in the younger grades, stories, excerpts from the daily press, a brief opening talk by a pupil, a wall newspaper, or the group's "question box" may open the discussion. An important source for the formation of direct impressions, discussions, and debates is the annual week-long visit to other places with a different way of life, as well as visits to other schools. The criterion for the success of a debate is whether the pupils continue the discussion among themselves and with the educator once the formal meeting is over.

Despite all these projects and tools, ideological education encounters difficulties that are inherent in kibbutz education and also manifest themselves in the prevailing skeptical attitude of Israeli youth toward political parties and organized politics in general. But the major difficulty stems from the fact that the youth are being educated, within the kibbutz secondary school and kibbutz society, in a way of life that offers ample spheres of interest and challenges for young people, leaving little energy for outside events. The visits, organized by the youth movement or the school itself, to places where a different way of life is seen—a cooperative village (moshav), a newly developed town, an Arab village, a kibbutz affiliated with a different movement, or a city factory—arouse interest and stimulate critical thinking. However, the intensive life of the kibbutz high school itself puts all these into the background, creating a problem that we are trying to overcome in our educational work.

Even more fundamental than the above-described difficulty is the fact that these young people are the second generation living in the kibbutz. For the founders of our movement, the very idea of a kibbutz was a revolutionary concept that altered the very basis of their lives. This personal revolution helped them to establish a radical cognitive approach to every societal problem, even those outside the kibbutz. For our sons, however, born and raised in the kibbutz, it is first and foremost a practical reality. The kibbutz, with its scale of values, its way of life, is loved and taken for granted. The kibbutz ideology becomes part of the personality of the young person who grows up in it, but it does not in itself stimulate him to struggle, to radical thinking, or to zealous devotion to a cause. While the average kibbutz youth shows a greater interest in political events and is perhaps better equipped to deal with current affairs in a more principled and critical way than most young people elsewhere, only a relatively small proportion are motivated by an enthusiastic dedication to their cause, as was the case with the first generation of settlers. Some of them believe that since "pioneering," Zionism, and socialism have been fully achieved within the kibbutz, they need no longer be attracted to any public activity outside kibbutz life. We realize that their emotional ties to the kibbutz have a positive impact, but they also create the danger of narrowing one's horizons. There is a hazard that our young people will be "temporary intellectuals" only in their youth, and leave behind them the spark of critical thinking and ideological motivation as they embark on their adult lives. We consider this dangerous because the kibbutz as a social movement cannot continue to exist in an environment that is different—even hostile—in the economic, social, and spiritual sense unless it wages a struggle as an ideological-political movement.

The problems confronting us in ideological education arise not only from the fact that our sons belong to the second generation in a firmly established kibbutz village, but also from the trends common to contemporary youth the world over, our country included. Obviously, there is no foundation to such generalizations about the character of present-day youth as "the generation of silent skepticism" or "the youth who have rejected all ideologies"—witness the ferment among students and other youth circles in Western and Eastern Europe and in the United States. Nevertheless, until the Six-Day War of 1967, wide circles of Israeli youth manifested a marked disassociation from all general social ideologies and gave much more preference to individualistic approaches (except for problems of security and national solidarity).

The situation has changed with recent events: the focus of young

people's interest since the Six-Day War and the events preceding it has
been the problem of security and peace. Keenly aware of developments,
they follow them with tension and manifest a profound identification
with the stand taken by the Israeli people and the Israel Defense Forces.
This has led to a rise in political awareness—newspapers are read hungrily,
and heated discussions take place on how peace can be achieved and on
possible perspectives for the future of the country. Nevertheless it is
significant to note that, conjoined with spontaneous manifestations of
fear and even outbursts of hatred, particularly among the younger age
groups, there have been few displays of chauvinism. In a survey conducted among the graduating class of high school students (17- and
18-year-olds), the majority said that they hated the Arab leadership and
the terrorists but not the Arab people, and that the movement's slogan of
"brotherhood of nations" still stands today. At the same time, they
noted the need to maintain military preparedness for any emergency that
might arise.

This response is not only the result of our movement's education and
political stand, but is also undoubtedly influenced by the attitudes of
those young people from the three kibbutz movements who fought in
the Six-Day War. In the anthology *Fighters Talk,* which includes recol-
lections of fighting men and their thoughts after the battle was over, we
find that they identify with the aims of the campaign and readily accept
the obligation to fulfill their duty (in practice, many went beyond the
call of duty). There is, however, no trace of exhilaration or joy in
fighting; instead, we find disgust at war's inevitable brutality. The desire
to win the war and stay alive has not engendered feelings of hatred for
the enemy. In their encounters with the vanquished enemy and with
civilians, these young ex-soldiers feel deeply that war does not wipe out
fundamental humanitarian principles. In this way the young people of
the kibbutzim—like thousands of other soldiers in Israel's Defense
Forces—have proved that the ideological education they received and the
kibbutz atmosphere in which they were reared have instilled in them
social and humanitarian principles which have, for most of them, with-
stood the terrible, inhuman ordeal of war.

The areas of Jewish and socialist education are more complex. In
connection with the former, in our ideological education we must first
take into account an attitude of estrangement on the part of Sabras from
their brothers in the diaspora. True, this feeling changed somewhat after
the Six-Day War, as a result of the wave of solidarity with Israel that
swept world Jewry. However, it still remains an educational and psychological problem, especially in nonreligious circles.

A problem that is relevant to kibbutz education, and to the political left-wing organization of the kibbutz movement in particular, is that of socialist education. In the first place, it is natural that the constant danger and tension we face have increased feelings of national solidarity and weakened alertness to social differences. No less decisive in this realm is the effect of the crisis of socialist ideology the world over (beginning with the revelations of the Twentieth Communist Party Congress in the Soviet Union). The tendency to reject, or at best to be indifferent to, socialist ideology has been deepened by the attitude of the Soviet government toward Israel and Russian Jews, by the hostility of most of the New Left to Israel, and by the reactionary character of Arab socialism. The blurring of the lines between socialism versus the welfare state, and a socialist party versus a social democratic party, have also contributed—at first in the case of adults and later with adolescents—to the discrediting of organized brands of socialism and to skepticism regarding the possibility of ever achieving a genuine humanistic socialism.

The educator of today's kibbutz youth can no longer hope to instill socialist attitudes in his pupils by merely presenting established socialist principles as absolute truths, nor can he advocate blind solidarity with all socialist countries. Instead, he should attempt to cultivate a general sensitivity to human problems and a critical dialectical way of thinking. He should also try to convey the view that socialism has nowhere reached its final stage, but must now redefine its premises on the basis of past lessons; socialism should not be expected only to answer questions, but, like any other theory and way of life, should raise new ones. This approach, while it is sometimes unattractive to youth who seek clear-cut answers and unequivocal beliefs, is still the only viable way to imbue young people with an awareness of, and an interest in, theory, for in the kibbutz there is a constant interaction between social reality and theory.

There is, however, a singular asset to ideological education: the contrast between the socialist achievements of the kibbutz community (equality of opportunity, a high level of mutual aid, etc.) and the inequality, oppression, and other wrongs prevailing in many societies, including, to a lesser degree, Israeli society. These contrasts can sometimes clarify social questions better than any dramatic event outside the children's experience, and should be emphasized by the educator whenever possible. He should also link his pupil's emotional identity with the socialist-humanistic values of their kibbutz to a broader philosophical outlook, one that will enable them to relate to problems of world magnitude. One must remember, though, that as long as Israel remains in its present state of physical struggle for existence, national issues will be a primary concern and social questions will remain somewhat in the background. The strong feelings of national solidarity, which understandably thrive at such a time, should be broadened by the educator to encompass feelings of solidarity with the Jewish people all over the world. Finally, the educator must guide his pupils—particularly at such times—to prevent them from losing their capacity for critical social thinking and to develop in them a deep inner longing for peace.

Clearly, kibbutz educators cannot provide solutions for all these problems. Our other means of ideological education include free discussion with those holding conflicting views, so that young people can become aware of all sides of an issue and develop a keen alertness to matters that concern the general public. Aside from this intellectual confrontation, we believe that most children in the upper grades of high school—other than those who have been working as youth movement leaders in small towns and settlements in the vicinity of their kibbutz—should engage in social work among the youth and adults of the new immigrant villages: helping out in youth clubs, combating illiteracy, and in other ways coming into contact with what has come to be called "the other Israel" and its problems. This will have the effect of creating active, close contacts between high school pupils and their environment, and with the new immigrants in particular. Such encounters are bound to increase the likelihood of future social involvement by young people.

Beyond this, their future alertness and activity will depend to no small extent on their integration into the kibbutz as full-fledged members. The recruiting of young kibbutz members for high school teaching jobs and other educational tasks, and the gradual integration of this generation in positions of responsibility within the movement, open up new possibilities for intensifying ideological-political education among the youth. For example, political projects sponsored by the League of Young Members in Kibbutz Artzi—action against religious coercion, campaigning for the abolition of military rule in the Arab sector (before the Six-Day War), etc.—resulted in greater political interest among the older pupils even though they did not actively participate in the campaign.

In recent years we have witnessed, among those who have returned from the Army and among pupils in the higher grades of high school, a revival of intellectual and social interest. There seems to be more concern about the social gap between Oriental and Western Jews, and young people are asking themselves what they can do about it. Conjoined with a commitment to problems of security, they seek a peaceful solution to the conflict and to the fate of the Arab population in Israel.

The egocentric outlook of some young people regarding the future, and their disapproval of clear-cut ideological answers given by the older generation, answers which they claim do not fit the problems and the mentality of our times, have created the setting for a fresh look at the personal and social meaning of kibbutz life. This recent tendency has been expressed in the formation of small discussion groups and in tentative positions about the new situation. These are only the first new trends and involve a small minority, but they may later turn out to be the catalyst for an ideological reinterpretation of the basic values of the kibbutz movement.

Further cultivation of the ideological sphere requires alertness and devotion on the part of our educators. We must continue to link the idea and its implementation in life—the only guarantee that the intellectual and moral values of the young person will become an integral part of his developing personality.

Education for Work

Beginning with the upper grades of elementary school, work becomes a regular feature in the life of the nine- or ten-year-old—about 30 minutes a day. By the time he is in the upper classes of high school, about two hours are allocated daily.

The work of high school pupils is important for the kibbutz, particularly during seasons of manpower shortage. However, in addition to economic considerations, the children's work in their own kibbutz has an educational value: it expresses the kibbutz society's wish to instill an appreciation of the human and social value of physical work. We attempt to inculcate in our students an attitude which attaches a social significance to labor, respect for the various types of work necessary for the kibbutz to exist, a personal interest in the advancement of the sector in which they work, and a feeling of satisfaction in joining in the solution of problems that arise in work.

We stress to our children, even the younger ones, the moral aspect of work, and teach them that the individual can both fulfill his civic duty to his kibbutz and find personal development and satisfaction through work. We point out, too, that in the kibbutz there is no economic exploitation of one person by another—a principle that fits in with the broader social outlook of the kibbutz, which sees the value of the kibbutz village, based as it is on creative work, as a part of the realization of the Zionist-Socialist ideal. The national and social revival of the Jewish people is possible only by a normalization of the vocational structure of society, which means a radical departure from the structure of Jewish society abroad as well as from the marked trend of the Israeli people today to enter commercial and liberal professions. In contrast, we seek an integration of spiritual creativity and physical work, and we reject the notion that there must be a conflict between the two.

Despite the great value attached to work by the kibbutz educational system, the curriculum is geared to providing a general—not a vocational—education. The general fundamentals of knowledge and the techniques of learning, we believe, are the basic means of enabling students to adjust to their future work. And in view of the rapid pace of technological progress, both in mechanized kibbutz agriculture and in growing kibbutz industrialization, that work will require constant learning.

The emphasis on work and study in our educational system expresses itself in many ways—for example, scientific knowledge in agriculture is stressed through the teaching of botany and chemistry. Prevocational subjects have recently been introduced in the senior classes of high school; this will allow pupils to choose between vocations in agriculture, agrotechnics, the economic services, education, and technology. Four hours per week (out of a total of 36 hours of class study) will be devoted to these subjects, and will include periods of practical work in shops and laboratories as well as time for theoretical study. The purpose of prevocational program is to lay the general foundations for the profession chosen by the student and to complement his work in that branch during his last two years at school.

High school students work every day throughout their studies, with the number of hours determined by age. The younger classes work on the children's farm of the high school under the guidance of adults and older children. The farm, which is larger than the one in the children's society, also has small repair workshops. The students are responsible for the landscape gardening and for the maintenance of the school grounds.

As a training and experimental facility, the children's farm is not necessarily profitable. It is a small-scale undertaking, and the level of mechanization is low compared to other kibbutz enterprises. Its central goal is to help the young child to understand the general structure and work of a farm, and to feel personally responsible for the branch in which he works, be it a small plot or some animals under his care. In his two final years, every student opts for one branch in the kibbutz economy and works there most of the time.

Work in the branch has a twofold importance: first, the student participates in the everyday life of the adults, thus reducing the danger of a unilateral withdrawal of adolescents among themselves; second, the fact that their work is so vital to the kibbutz economy—a truth of which they are well aware—and that their work responsibility is geared to individual capabilities gives them the feeling that, even while they are still at school, they are part of a society that needs them. This may be one reason why the tendency to a "moratorium" during adolescence—to use Erikson's term—when most social obligations are put off until adulthood, is not as prevalent in the kibbutz as elsewhere.

However, even this organic growth in a life of work does not always fortify the young person against possible conflicts between his own individual tendencies and the needs and opportunities of the kibbutz; but the practical link he has formed with work in a branch of his own choosing, and the set of values instilled in him, are important factors in his doubts, hesitations, and decisions. We have the impression that satisfaction in their work and vocational progress is for our youngsters a more important expression of self-realization than it was to the older generation, who saw in the building of new branches a more general challenge.

The problem is sometimes more severe for the girls because of the growing mechanization of agriculture, which had employed many women in the past. Since women had traditionally occupied positions in education and in services which have not changed with respect of manpower requirements, they have increasingly concentrated in these areas of employment. The range of professions open to girls has been greatly reduced. Deliberations on how to extend this range through general planning are now under way in the entire kibbutz movement. The development of industry in the kibbutzim opens up new possibilities, but it still falls short of a fully satisfactory solution.

The objective requirements of vocational advancement and the individual's wish for further training have in recent years increased the willingness of kibbutzim to send their sons and daughters to vocational courses after completion of military training. Some go to the Kibbutz Teacher Training College (either to two-year courses for child nurses or to three-year courses for school and kindergarten teachers), others to the Agriculture College, and a smaller number to the university for academic studies. In 1971, more than 100 young kibbutzniks studied at different universities.

The availability of channels for professional advancement—following the mature choice of a branch of work—heightens the need for a general education combined with practical work as a prerequisite for a well-rounded kibbutz life. Despite some shortcomings a decisive majority of

our high school graduates are integrated into their kibbutzim, and kibbutz education can be credited with positive achievements in this connection.

Relationships with Parents During Adolescence

At all stages of kibbutz education, the family is regarded as a vital
element in the healthy development of the child. The degree of harmony
in his relationships with his parents and with his communal children's
home largely determines the success or failure of his entire education.
From his earliest days, the child derives security and love from both of
these interesting spheres. By encouraging his practical and mental autonomy, both are instrumental in developing a feeling of independence
even before sexual awakening in puberty. Relations with parents, educators, and fellow members of one's group form a vital psychological
basis that influences future relations with the social environment and
with the objective world.

While we agree with the postulate that the age of puberty is not an
automatic, mechanical progression from previous stages but is, rather, a
stage of development in its own right, one that molds the character traits
of the individual, it is evident that the course of development in this new
stage is dependent upon the previous stages and that the first "magic
years" play a special role.

Adolescence, in the psychological literature, is generally described as a
period of sharp clashes and conflicts between youth and parents. It is
explained as the revival of the Oedipus situation which once again—
following the calm latency period—arouses ambivalent feelings toward
one's parents. This ambivalence, at a time of sexual awakening, consists
of a need for renewed psychological relations of dependence together
with a longing for greater independence and a wish to disassociate oneself
from hitherto unquestioned rules and arrangements of living and education.

The sharp emotional conflict characteristic of this age caused us to
anticipate—even in our society—an adolescent rebellion that might be
directed against parents and the established societal values they represent, while still relying on such examples as the Jewish pioneer youth
movement of the previous generation and the "rebels without cause" of
contemporary times. However, the kibbutz movement has not yet undertaken a sufficiently well-formulated psychological research project to
enable us to present a theory concerning adolescence under the con-

ditions of kibbutz education. Based on the experience of many of our educators and parents, the relations between kibbutz parents and their adolescent children are no different from those on the outside.

In most instances, surface relations with parents do not assume the character of external rebelliousness and internal rejection, but that of greater psychological distance, an unwillingness on the part of the adolescent to talk at home about his personal affairs, his situation in the group, and his first erotic experiences. However, he is generally willing—and is appreciative of the opportunity—to discuss his studies, his work, his opinions about the kibbutz and external, cultural, political, and other affairs, and his plans for the future.

There is no lack of minor parent-adolescent conflicts (also found in preadolescent groups) on matters of health, dress, esthetic taste, and so on. However, since the parents do not have the principal educational responsibility, parent-child relations are for the most part fundamentally smooth. True, one no longer sees the direct emotional display of positive feelings toward parents, as when the children were younger. On the other hand, disrespectful behavior is quite rare. This ambivalent attitude to parents does not signify all-out rejection; the children are still interested in maintaining good relations and are sensitive about them, as can be seen from their regular visits to their parents' quarters.

During adolescence the parental influence is transferred more to the realm of the conscious. The atmosphere in the parents' home, their tastes, the kind of music they play, the books that interest them, their views on various issues, and their cultural horizons and direction—all these have a considerable impact on the spiritual and cultural development of the adolescent. These influences, together with other factors, help to mold the young person's character.

This is not to say that there are no cases of opposition to parental attitudes. Opposition can take the form of adopting a different style of clothing, or a greater interest in nonclassical radio music (such as "hit parade"), or assuming a critical approach to ideals which the parents cherish—signs of the adolescents' need for emancipation from their parents, yet interwoven with a feeling of identification.

If we try to understand the nature of these relations and why they are so different from those generally described in the psychological literature, we may find the solution not so much in the educational capabilities of parents, which of course vary greatly between individuals, but rather in the unique situation of the young person being reared in kibbutz conditions. The decisive factor here is that the young person is not under parental supervision with regard to minor, everyday activities. The inevitable conflicts bound to arise are more likely to occur in the less affective area of relations with others of his own age or with his educators. The group, together with the children's society whose rules he must accept, form a body with which he can identify and whose authority he finds easier to accept or oppose. These factors influence the pattern of relationships—and the nuances in the direct personal contacts created—between our young people and their parents.

However, several more specific characteristics are decisive for this age group. While the attitude to parents is a very personal matter, adolescents do regard their parents as part of the generation of kibbutz founders or as that generation which has the current responsibility for its existence. These adults symbolize a way of life: in their lives and opinions they represent social, moral, and political values with which our young people basically identify—even if they tend toward differences in style and emphasis. Herein lies the source of the parents' influence in molding the philosophy and values of their children.

The weaker ambivalence in the attitude of the young person toward his parents is also due to the fact that he does not, as a matter of course, see evidence of the intimate aspects of relations between his parents. Nor is he confronted with their behavior in everyday life—at work and in the company of others. Possibly this separation from the daily routines of parents preserves a certain degree of idealization, even at this age of "idol-debunking." A more realistic evaluation of their own parents is generally attained later—after military service—when the young people are accepted as full-fledged members of the kibbutz. Only then do they really get to know the kibbutz members and their characteristics, as becomes evident in everyday situations. However, even when the naive and uncritical childhood identification with parents and with the kibbutz gives way in youth to a more critical evaluation, and even when, as young kibbutz members, they sometimes feel a great gap between themselves and the older generation in terms of aspirations, style, manner of speech and action, etc., these relations still do not assume an affective familial character; rather, they are set in the context of relations between the different age groups of the adult society.

We have found that in many families, particularly where parents allow their adolescent children a wide range of autonomy and freedom, there is a revival of a close relationship between the generations, particularly when the offspring themselves become parents. We even see deep attachments in a "three-generation family." Such phenomena are possible only where there is absolutely no economic dependence between parents and children, and where the educational policy creates a sound climate for all age groups to be able to achieve this kind of relationship. The educational regime of adolescents combines the elements of distance and confrontation, of youthful activity for its own sake and goals, and of freedom and spiritual and educational authority, including a philosophical outlook regarding the future. The main advantage apparently lies in the fact that relations between parents and children develop within a society that can offer its children a set of moral and personal values as a practical way of life embodying these values.

Relationships with the Kibbutz, the Adult Society, and Self-Realization

The attitude of young people to their own kibbutz is nurtured by the fact that, until the age of 12 or 13, they live in the kibbutz—they know its members, every tree and stone, and the surrounding area. They carry with them to high school strong and meaningful associations and lifelong memories.

When they reach secondary school, where studies and social activities are conducted away from their home kibbutz, they experience a certain feeling of tenseness, a longing for the security of home combined with a sense of distance. In our view, this relative remoteness from the everyday life of the kibbutz has educational advantages: it prevents premature imitation of adult life and safeguards the value of studies and youthful activity.

Of course, daily encounters with kibbutz members enable the youngsters to get to know their parents' friends and neighbors. In some cases the familiarity and contact engender a feeling of "group relatives." There are also relationships with adult kibbutz members at the permanent place of work chosen by the individual youngster.

The attitude to the veterans, to the generation of "fathers," however, is one of relative remoteness. The young person does not form close ties, or seek persons with whom to identify, among this age group. Closer and more friendly relations are formed between high school seniors and those who have completed their Army service—the students of yesterday. There is a keen interest in the progress of former school graduates, at first in the Army and later in the kibbutz. When the Army returnees seek an adjustment to kibbutz life, they serve as a catalyst for the students, stimulating a questioning and critical attitude and assuming a leadership role.

In the secondary school the pupil, like the kibbutz member in adult society, encounters a multitude of styles and philosophical outlooks that reach out to him through the press, the radio, and films, through visits to friends in the city, and through group visits to different parts of the country. Even though the kibbutz remains the decisive, normative factor in their lives, the young people experience conflicts as a result of their contact with so many varied groups and their exposure to the clash between the social, moral, and esthetic values represented by the kibbutz and the surrounding environment. The child's personality is partly determined by his view of kibbutz procedures as an adult society, one that is based on clearly defined principles and ways of life. The young person becomes aware of the continuity in the kibbutz and the differences between the generations. His relationships—with the adult world, on the one hand, and with the peer group on the other—form the specific background of the kibbutz adolescent in his search for identity and self-realization.

"Self-realization"—as defined particularly by Erikson—signifies a search for the meaning of life, the aspiration to do something creative that will in some way leave the individual's imprint on the world around him and effect changes in some part of it. But there can be no healthy personal identity that is not in some way linked to the individual's identification with a wider group and with an idea that goes beyond the personal. Personal and social aspects constitute a dialectical whole, but in reality this unity sometimes breaks up into conflicting elements. Education should, among other things, equip its subjects with two ostensibly opposing characteristics: the aspiration for a broad and comprehensive personal and social perspective, and the ability to make decisions in accordance with a set of values.

We aspire to inculcate in our adolescent students, in accordance with the changing needs of age, a growing sense of personal and spiritual independence—autonomy in one's private affairs and respect for this same autonomy in others. When our youth have completed their schooling and are about to begin military service, they should be able to envisage—in broad outlines at least—a personal perspective of their future in the kibbutz.

These trends toward strengthening individual self-knowledge and autonomy in the educational sphere and in the life of the kibbutz environment inevitably run into difficulties that are specific to the communal way of life. The situation becomes quite complex in the later adolescent years, since at this age the closely knit framework of the group can interfere with the individual's need for privacy, especially because the adolescent's social sense and self-control are not yet sufficiently developed. The group still occupies the focal position in the consciousness of the students. During the last year of school, however, we sometimes hear complaints about too much togetherness, and attempts are made to redefine the boundaries of group attachment. The process of spiritual severance from the group is a slow one, occasionally culminating in a crisis when the individual finds himself in the new and unfamiliar environment of the Army. This is a further important step toward the crystallization of his awareness of himself as an individual who is also a kibbutz member.

A frequently raised problem, one that has a direct bearing on the questions of the self-realization of our young people concerns personal decision-making. The likelihood that our children will return to the kibbutz upon completion of their Army service is too much taken for granted. True, almost all those born and reared in the kibbutz do return. But the question of future membership in the kibbutz becomes an issue only during the initial period after his return, for he must now put his hopes and plans to a practical test, and these hopes and plans may clash with the interests of the community as a whole. The "test" may involve a job that is offered him, the attitude of the kibbutz toward the course of studies he has chosen, a marriage partner who is not from his own kibbutz and does not wish to live in his kibbutz, or any other personal dilemma.

If the young person finds that he is at odds with the kibbutz community and with the possibilities it offers him, his decision will be made on the basis of the relative force of the values he has acquired throughout his education and the degree of attraction his personal aims hold for him. Such a situation is liable to recur several times, in relation to different types of conflict, and the option between settling down in the kibbutz and leaving it may not be decided at any one given moment, but become subject of reconsideration. The basic assumption, nevertheless, is that the majority of the younger generation will remain in their home kibbutz. Only in this way will the kibbutz village community become a permanent way of life.

The young person's path to self-realization, a highly complex and ongoing process, does not end when his formal schooling is over. But the kibbutz high school is a decisive stage along the path of formulating ideas and values and identifying with a group and with ideological objectives.

The individual may undergo a crisis in the Army, where, cut off from his group and his previous environment, he finds himself surrounded by people with radically different ideas and concepts. Later, when he returns to the kibbutz, he may experience readjustment difficulties after having absorbed some of the attidues of the outside, attitudes that are often not in harmony with the values and way of life of the kibbutz. Some of our youth do not immediately settle down in their home kibbutz after military service; they may opt for a "third year's service"— assistance organized by the movement for struggling new kibbutzim—or for work in the youth movement. Those who gain the experience of such activity tend to go back to their kibbutzim with greater awareness and acceptance.

Some of our young people, despite deep roots in kibbutz society— even if they are not the type who forever "search for identity"—form their personalities only after conflicts, sacrifices, and deliberate choices between different scales of values. After all, the true meaning of choice and freedom involves the concept of giving up something for the sake of something else, choosing between contrasting possibilities, each with its own attractions. According to Rappaport, each society determines its own scale of values for the sake of which a certain price is paid.

In many ways, the path to self-realization is more complex for our children than it was for their parents. Under present kibbutz conditions, self-realization is a more conscious process, demanding of our young people more specific and realistic answers than it did of the kibbutz founders (for whom the actual creation of the kibbutz was synonymous with a highly defined personal identity). Nevertheless, we believe that despite all the differences between our children and ourselves, they will— *in their own way*—find a way to integrate their kibbutz values and motivations with the desire for satisfying legitimate personal yearnings.

The kibbutz has always attempted to merge close community life with individual development. Until recently, in part for historical reasons, the emphasis was placed more on the collective side; but the economic and social progress of the kibbutz has now enabled the second generation to express a more conscious yearning for individuality. We cannot foresee what the final outcome of this new trend will be, but the process of redefining the relation between these two basic elements of kibbutz life is undoubtedly under way.

Stability and Change

With the passage of years, changes evolved in kibbutz education and, in particular, in the education of adolescents. Most of these changes were due to the development of the kibbutz movement—demographic, economic, social, and ideological. Progress in all these spheres was so rapid that people began to question all past methods and educational customs, and the ensuing discussions led to continuing innovations in our educational approaches to various subjects: a view of the kibbutz as a cooperative society; the role of the kibbutz in the larger Zionist struggle; the construction of a socialist society in Israel; the relationship of the kibbutz to nonkibbutz society in Israel; the inner development of the kibbutz; and relations between the generation within the kibbutz and the movement as a whole.

Whether the kibbutz will be able to adjust to necessary technological and administrative changes without adverse affects on its social principles, and whether the rise of the standard of living will not turn it into a consumer society, constitute key factors in the education of adolescents. It is precisely this age group whose reactions are a very sensitive seismograph of changes in the adult society. Of course, even though recognizing the problems is not identical with being able to solve them, we hope that open-mindedness and honest discussions will provide some guarantee that the kibbutz movement and its educational methods will not develop spontaneously.

The second factor we have mentioned—the internal development of the kibbutz—is no less dynamic than the first, and its influence upon our system of education is necessarily far-reaching. In the past five to ten years, the older kibbutz has undergone a turbulent development because of demographic changes. It was practically revolutionized by absorbing the second generation as members, but it has also absorbed new contingents from the cities of Israel and from abroad. The membership of dozens of kibbutzim has grown from 250 to 400, with the total population in each kibbutz now about 500 to 700. The kibbutz has changed from a society with a homogeneous age grouping to a three-generation society, and most kibbutzim have been able to expand their agricultural branches and their industry at a rapid rate.

The status of the family has also undergone considerable change. Its social role has increased, as has its involvement in the education of children. The wide prevalence of the extended three-generation family has created a warmer and more sociable climate for the individual, the family, and its members. These factors have helped to correct former educational distortions, such as the austere limitations on the amount of time parents were permitted to spend with their children. In fact, there has been a complete turnabout, with parents now in contact with their children for many hours each day—a demonstration of the strength and flexibility of a socialist economy and society, based on inner freedom and democracy.

Changes in the role of the family and the increase in its social power require, with every new generation, a clarification of the interaction of three basic educational factors: the kibbutz society, the family, and the educational system. The functions of each must be redefined, and discussions on educational policies must be updated. Even though our society's amenability to change brings an ever-increasing stream of new problems, on the whole it enriches our lives and raises our social level.

The role of the younger generation in the kibbutz, and the relations between the generations, undoubtedly exercise a strong and direct influence on the youth, particularly on adolescents. Children born in the kibbutz are now becoming the parents of adolescent children, and it is they who will, in the course of time, determine the character of adolescent education.

The integration of the generations confronts the kibbutz with many new and sometimes complicated problems. Despite this, Kibbutz Artzi has successfully managed to integrate, as full-fledged members, more than 70 percent of those born in its settlements who completed their education there. This is particularly noteworthy in an area characterized by general migration from village to town and by a widening gap between the scales of values of different generations, and can be attributed not only to the educational system but also to the social character of the kibbutz and its objectives. The essential nature of the kibbutz, aside from differences of form and style, has created a common basis in mode of life and principles that still permits considerable leeway to the individual members within the overall framework.

The integration of large numbers of young people in our educational institutions—as educators, childern's nurses, and youth movement leaders—has prompted a reexamination of various problems among the staff. The fact that the age gap between educators and their charges is now smaller facilitates the educational influence of the former and promotes a better rapport between both groups.

The dynamic changes in the kibbutz manifest themselves not only in a planned and harmonious manner, but also in the form of contradictions and conflicts. Any given standard or custom becomes problematic once it fails to meet actual social needs, just as any given ideological formula becomes unacceptable when it no longer corresponds to present realities. Recent developments have indeed enriched kibbutz life, but at the same time new problems have been created in connection with organizational patterns and with making adjustments to the increased size of the settlements.

We have dwelt at some length on the difficulties arising from the specific form of the kibbutz educational system for adolescents. To complete the picture and place it in its proper perspective, it would be appropriate to mention certain difficulties which are frequently encountered among nonkibbutz youth in general, but which do not occupy our educational staff because of their rareness. We find almost no manifestations of juvenile delinquency at our educational institutions nor are there behavior problems arising from boredom or lack of interest. We have no examples of angry rebellion against the educational environment, its values, and the way of life it represents. And there are few cases of perversion, homosexuality, or sexual deviation (we believe that such cases of personal difficulties require the help of a psychologist).

The fact that we hardly have to cope with problems of this nature, which today weigh so heavily on many educators outside the kibbutz, cannot be attributed only to the high quality of our educators. In our opinion, the situation is evidence of the success of the fundamental factors in our education—the relatively wide and activating autonomy of the children's community, and the relative harmony between the three fundamental components of our approach: identification with the values of kibbutz society, a guiding and demanding approach by the educators, and positive relations between parents and children.

Education must be open to change, but it requires a climate of relative stability and continuity in which innovations are carefully examined lest they turn out to be mere passing fads—indeed, as the saying goes, "Do not discard the old just for the sake of the new."

We believe that this combination—the educational staff's firm loyalty, each to its own kibbutz; the sense of belonging to the broader movement's educational personnel; an open-mindedness and a readiness to learn; and a loyal, abiding identification with the principles of the kibbutz and its collective education—offers the key to dynamic continuity of our educational enterprise.

maximum concentration of the pupil's interest and effort

Methods of
Study and Instruction
in High School

by Zvi Lavi

The first children's society of Hashomer Hatzair was set up in Bet Alpha in 1924-25. Its founders had no experience, no knowledge of psychology, no pedagogical theory. Two powerful forces nourished their educational work from the very beginning and infused these prioneering educators with a burning enthusiasm: (1) the kibbutz society; and (2) the youth movement experience of Hashomer Hatzair.

The kibbutz was still a new phenomenon, although a few kvutzot were relatively well established. Despite many difficulties and disappointments, the settlers had profound faith, and it was only natural that this atmosphere should influence the children and their educators. The walls separating the school from the kibbutz, and the teachers from the community at large, gave way—life burst into the school. Even after the first birth pangs had subsided, the kibbutz continued to influence the development of the basic principles of the educational system of Kibbutz Artzi.

The second factor which left its imprint on the education of youth from the very beginning was the practical experience of the Hashomer Hatzair youth movement. Confidence in young people and a serious attitude toward them; interest in the special problems and uncertainties of adolescence; the attempt to guide and influence youth in informal ways; belief in the independence and responsibility of youth; and, most important, the idea of the independent peer group—all these elements still influence secondary education in Kibbutz Artzi, and all of them originated in the youth movement.

Nevertheless, it became clear that neither the influence of the kibbutz alone nor the educational experience of the youth movement was a sufficiently firm foundation for our educational enterprise. The lack of a psychological and educational theory, and of a clear-cut pedagogical and didactic pattern, was felt. The third factor contributing to the project method in Kibbutz Artzi was the ideas of modern education of the time, and the example of the progressive and pioneering schools which attempted to put these ideas into practice throughout the world.

It was no accident that the founders of the kibbutz education, in their search for an educational and psychological theory that would harmonize with kibbutz principles and world outlook, turned to educational theories which negated the traditional methods of mechanical drill, the view of the child as a passive object who must be stuffed full of information, the system of punishments and rewards, etc.

Several of the newest and most daring educational ideas were absorbed so organically into the kibbutz reality that one finds it extremely difficult to determine which was the more decisive factor—these philosophies of education or the social structure of the kibbutz—in the development of several of the educational patterns prevalent today. The integration of the two elements is illustrated in the questions that follow.

Education for all children until the age of 18, as it obtains in the kibbutz movement today. Is this principle the fruit of modern educational thought, which strives to give an education to all youth (but is still far from the realization of the principle), or is it a social necessity stemming from the conditions of kibbutz life?

The children's and youth societies, as practiced in various forms in the entire kibbutz movement. Does this stem from the influence of modern pedagogical trends, or is it simply natural and self-explanatory within the framework of the kibbutz?

Abolition of grading and report cards in Kibbutz Artzi

schools. Is this merely carrying a daring educational idea into practice (incidentally, a practice unique to the kibbutz movement), or is it due to the absence of competition in kibbutz society and to the emphasis placed on equality and cooperation?

Integration of physical labor in the school's daily schedule. This pedagogical principle has been emphasized since the days of Pestalozzi, but is it possible to imagine youth in the kibbutz not participating in one way or another in farm work?

From these few examples, it is clear that the linking of the kibbutz factor with progressive education in our system is organic and not in the least accidental.

The philosophy of progressive education, however, does contain ideas and methods that could not be adapted to kibbutz education, regardless of their objective merit. The most outstanding example is the opinion, held by many progressive educators, that one should not educate toward any clearly defined social and political goals. According to this view, one should point out different possible directions and leave the student free to decide when he grows up. Within the framework of this article, we shall not attempt an overall refutation, although we feel that such "freedom of choice" is basically wrong. However, it should be quite clear that kibbutz education cannot accept such a philosophy since, by its very nature, it is a directed education aimed at preparing its children for kibbutz life and perpetuating the existence and growth of the kibbutz movement.

To force young people to adopt the opinions of their educators is certainly a faulty and useless method. They should be exposed to various ideas, approaches, and organizations for the purpose of developing their critical faculties and the ability to exercise independent judgment. Our education is ideologically directed, and it is not neutral. Let us suggest some practical consequences of this approach: an obligatory curriculum determined by adults; the influence of adult attitudes in the youth society; explicit ideological and political education; membership in the kibbutz as the central goal of education and instruction; etc.

In conclusion, we should not forget that the kibbutz, as a society which created the conditions for the realization of modern theories of education and instruction, and in practice laid new foundations in every area of life, not only absorbs new, revolutionary ideas of education, but serves as a discriminating strainer that allows certain ideas to pass through, and denies entrance to others.

It is well known that any practical change in an educational system raises numerous difficulties. In the case of revolutionary change, the obstacles are almost insurmountable: traditions and institutions, teachers with specific training and experience, and prejudices and material difficulties. Wherever new schools have arisen, they were connected with men of strong personal influence; but most of these schools could not survive when their founders were gone.

We do not want to create any illusions—even in the kibbutz movement the matter is not simple—but at least there are *objective conditions* which encourage and even require nontraditional and unconventional schools that are continually experimenting and searching.

In the present chapter, we shall trace the ideological and educational influences of modern psychology and pedagogy on the schools of Kibbutz Artzi.

Theoretical Origins of the Project Method

It is very important to distinguish between theories of education and educational institutions which attempt to put new ideas into practice. In order to bring about changes in the traditional and well-established educational order and to dare to experiment with new methods, many prerequisites are needed in addition to nice ideas. The history of education in the past two centuries bears witness to this fact. After World War I, revolutionary theories of education sprouted everywhere, but there were few experimental schools.

Three basic theoretical principles governed the kibbutz school at its beginnings:

1. Childhood and adolescence are not simply passing stages, preparatory to being an adult. Each is a definite period in life, with its own psychological set of laws. It is essential to study and to understand, on a scientific basis, the problems of growing up and the development at each stage, and to construct a new method of education and instruction.

2. The child or youth, not the teaching material, should occupy the center of educational concern and teaching activities. The goal of the school, therefore, must be the unifying and comprehensive education of the young person, taking into consideration all of his faculties. It must provide physical training, social and esthetic education, and, above all, every

opportunity and prerequisite for self-expression and creative work.

3. The child is active and dynamic by nature. Activity and real work constitute the soundest approach to effective learning. The school must provide the necessary facilities that will stimulate the child to initiative, work, and independent activities in many directions.

Despite countless attacks on progressive education, particularly on some of its distorted forms, when we examine the current pedagogical literature, we cannot help but recognize that many basic ideas of progressive education have retained their vitality. The main ideas in Jerome Bruner's *The Process of Education,* which have become the classic expression of educational trends in America today, are surprisingly close to some of the original ideas of progressive education (there are, of course, serious differences which we cannot discuss here).

Experimental Schools Which Influenced Us

Several schools which tried to practice revolutionary ideas of education and instruction had a marked influence on the evolution of our project method:

1. *The Dalton School,* founded and directed by the distinguished educator, Helen Parkhurst, in 1922. At this Massachusetts school the main stress was laid on the pupil's own activities and individual potentialities. The class was practically abolished, and studying was on an individual basis, with the teacher serving as guide.

The children were expected to achieve, each in his own way, certain norms in various subjects. There were separate rooms for each subject, where teachers gave the required guidance and advice. It is interesting to note that children generally worked for several days on one subject before switching to another. This proved that those who claimed there was too much fractionation in the traditional school were right, and that children tended to concentrate on one thing for a longer and uninterrupted period.

Eventually, special books were prepared at Dalton with instructions for the independent work of the child and his progress in every subject. This was the origin of the "books for independent work," so well known in our school, especially in the primary grades.

The Dalton system has outstanding advantages: individualization of the learning process; independent work and activity on the part of the pupil; and the setting of clear and achievable goals. There are, however, also disadvantages, the most important of which is neglect of the social aspect of learning, which enriches and offers intellectual and emotional stimulation which cannot otherwise be provided.

2. *The Winnetka School,* in a wealthy Chicago suburb, whose outstanding personality was Carlton Washburn (1925); in it, learning was based on two parallel processes:

a. Individualized study, as in the Dalton system, in which the pupil had to attain certain minimal achievements in basic subjects (reading, writing, arithmetic, history, geography). The goal was an active and socially conscious citizen.

b. Learning within the classroom on the basis of interest and individual inclination, without any predetermined plan. This part of the program was generally based on study projects from the children's everyday experience and environment. The disadvantage of the Winnetka system was the absence of an obligatory curriculum expressing the goals of the adult society for the education of the younger generation.

3. *Kilpatrick's (1925) project method.* The starting point of this method was the psychological world and the special interests of the child. The entire learning process was based upon the performance of a concrete task determined by the children—a project. In trying to accomplish their goal, they would encounter obstacles and difficulties which they had to overcome. They had to study the problems and turn to various sciences that could help them to find solutions. Here the teacher functions as guide, director, and assistant. When the subject is theoretically understood, the children arrive at the stage of practical performance and divide into groups. Each group carries out a definite part of the total task, and the results are presented to the entire class.

This method had a very important influence on our study projects in the younger grades. Its disadvantages, however, are striking: (1) the absence of a curriculum caused the chance selection of projects and left gaps in learning; (2) there is a danger that studies will seem less important than activity; and (3) the division of work enables the pupils to become expert in one area, to the complete neglect of other vital areas of knowledge.

In addition to the three major influences just discussed, there was also the *Arbeitsschule* (1920) of Georg Kerschensteiner and the school of P.P. Blonsky, which seemed especially suited to our conditions. The development of vocational schools influenced our farm youth, and we also studied the *Gesamtunterricht* (integrated curriculum) movement in Germany.

Principal Modifications of the Project Method

As the years passed, the educational undertaking of Kibbutz Artzi expanded and many new secondary schools were established. The entry of hundreds of new teachers, and the practical experience accumulated, brought many changes to the project method.

In the early days, the structure of the curriculum was very simple. The learning week (36 hours) contained four major study units: a project from the humanities, a science subject, foreign languages, and arts and crafts periods. The six daily lessons were usually divided among these four units. Two hours, including individual work, were devoted to each main project, and the remaining two hours were divided between languages (English, Arabic) and one of the arts (music, painting, handicrafts) or physical education. In the course of the year, three projects in the humanities and three science projects were covered, in compliance with a schematic curriculum. Mathematics was included in the time devoted to the natural sciences, although even from the beginning it was taught as a separate subject. The same was true of Hebrew language and grammar, which were taught within the framework of the humanities.

After World War II, when new secondary schools were established, it became the practice to convene teachers' conferences three times a year to discuss problems of education and instruction and to decide questions of policy. These summaries were looked upon as informal policy directives and accepted by all schools. Most of the modifications in the project method came about as a result of these conferences, although, of course, some changes have occurred naturally or by chance.

Following is a list of some of the principal modifications and their origins:

1. The necessity of devoting special attention to a number of *subjects and skills* was the first factor that led to modifications. Experience soon showed that the project method could not provide a satisfactory answer to all aspects of learning. Although there were apparent advantages in providing motivation and interest in the subject matter, stimulating the pupil to action, making the material concrete, and developing independent thought—all the elements which have been and still are neglected in the traditional school—it also became obvious that some subjects and skills are difficult to teach in a systematic way if they are not units in themselves. Some attempts to attach them to themes can succeed, but they are often very artificial. As a result, mathematics, language arts, crafts, and physical training were taken out of the project framework.

2. The most important revision was the standardization of the curriculum. Theoretically, we have never opposed a curriculum, as did several of the above-mentioned progressive schools of educational thought. During the early years, however, the curriculum had not yet taken form and existed only in outline. It was not specific enough to form a system. There were no pressures for achievement, and the few teachers we had were free to choose the project, its content, and the time to be spent on it. It was understood that neither formal achievement nor the quantity of information was primary; rather, depth of understanding, intellectual experiences, and acquisition of the ability for independent study were preferred. Therefore, the projects were very long and included considerable activity, independent study during lessons, summary booklets, exhibits, etc.

This lack of concern with formal achievement suffered when the course of study became crystallized and obligatory. Some of the immediate consequences were as follows:

a. Since it was necessary to limit the time devoted to each project in order to make room for subjects that seemed important for the curriculum, the first casualties were the written booklet summaries, exhibits, etc., all of which seemed less important than the subject matter itself.

b. The time devoted to independent study and individual work in the classroom was limited. At first this limitation affected the higher grades, where the pressure to "complete the subject matter" was felt most, but little by little this filtered down to the lower grades of secondary school.

c. As the pressure to achieve increased and the general level improved, difficulties arose. The gaps between various types of students widened, and it became more and more difficult to teach them all together. The introduction of several alternative courses of study in the higher grades is only one result of this problem.

d. As the educational level and requirements increased, specialization on the part of teachers became necessary and led to increased departmentalization, at first in the natural sciences. Science teachers were incapable of dealing with all of the subject matter in the various branches of science. Teachers specialized in the biological sciences or in physics and chemistry. A third division was soon introduced—agriculture. From the tenth grade on, teachers teach only their area of specialization. Among the humanities teachers, too, there are signs of similar specialization, mainly in literature and Bible study.

Over the years, some changes have occurred after serious discussion and conscious decisions at teachers' conferences and institutes; others were the result of practical difficulties, inadequate preparation of teachers, the inability to stand up to unjustified criticism from parents, etc. Nevertheless, as a whole, the project method has retained its vitality and educational advantages. Recent criticism of the traditional secondary school, and renewed awareness of the educational problems that beset the world today, can only strengthen our conviction that we have succeeded in protecting our secondary schools from convention and from the mad rush for formal achievement. We believe that our progressive methods of teaching combine vitality and flexibility.

Let us now discuss the actual pedagogical principles upon which our method is based and how they work out in practice.

Principles of Learning in the Secondary School (Ages 12-18)

In attempting to list the basic principles of our system of education and instruction, it is useful to distinguish between three kinds of principles: (1) the social-kibbutz principles of education; (2) general psychological and educational principles; and (3) specific principles of the project method.

At times there may be some overlapping of these principles, but they are qualitatively different. The educational principles of the first type, a direct consequence of the social structure of the kibbutz, are obvious even without any theory of psychology or education. For example, the teacher-pupil relationship is primarily the result of the relations between people in the kibbutz, specifically between adults and children. It is no accident that our kibbutz principles are identical, in many respects, with modern pedagogical principles.

The general psychological and educational principles are ones upon which every modern educational system and teaching method should be based. Emphasis on internal motivation and on the activity of the child is not necessarily connected with the project method, although this method has adopted these notions and tends to create learning situations which make their application easier.

The third group of principles is more specific and characteristic of the project method as formulated in the secondary schools of Kibbutz Artzi.

Social Principles. Nonselective Education

The sociological-pedagogical foundation of the educational system in Kibbutz Artzi—and, for that matter, in the entire kibbutz movement—is the premise that *all youth, without exception,* will remain within the educational framework until the *age of 18.* Some vital didactic and educational problems result from this premise. If individualization is a basic problem in education in general, it is even more cardinal in the kibbutz, which must ensure universal secondary education. Special consideration for both the gifted and for slow learners is only one aspect of the problem.

Universal education does not necessarily mean the same educational framework for all. On the contrary, to the extent that there is greater consideration for individual differences, specific abilities, and talents, the methods and external framework will be more flexible. Most important are the absence of selection in the usual sense—dropping out of school—and the ensuring of adequate opportunity to all.

Although, in individual cases, it may be necessary to create special conditions, the vast majority of adolescents can remain permanently within the home group, which is identical with the learning class. The study project plays a central role in the teaching process, for it provides the teacher with a variety of means to adapt the material and level to the individual needs of each student while at the same time maintaining a general framework for classroom discussion in which all can participate.

In the last two or three school years, the general framework of the project is proving to be inadequate. Our desire to provide education for all until the age of 18 requires more flexible learning situations in which all types of youth can find their place. A choice between various courses of study is an attempt to provide an answer to this problem. At present, the student selects 8 hours of a total of 36 in the school week; 3 of these are of a theoretical nature and 5 are practical. The theoretical courses may be chosen from mathematics-physics, biology, chemistry, literature, sociology and civics, Oriental studies, and art history. Prevocational training includes agromechanics, technology, education and psychology, agriculture, and home economics.

Sample Outline: Course in Oriental Studies

Aims of the course: becoming acquainted with the Arabs we meet daily in Israel, learning the history of the Arab people and of the neighboring countries.

Participants: 12 students from the eleventh and twelfth grades.

Time allotment: 8 hours per week—6 hours in the classroom and 2 hours for written work on a special project.

Course of study:

Unit I. Arabic history. Deals mainly with the pre-Islamic period, Islam, and the beginning of the Caliphates. Emphasis on human and social origins, customs, culture, etc. Comparison with the reality of the Arab world today.

Unit II. The Arab states today. Acquaints the student with several Arab countries—Syria, Iraq, Lebanon. The unit is based on individual student reports.

Unit III. Relations between Arabs and Jews, past and present. Contacts between the peoples, current problems, war and peace, etc.

In studying the Arabs in Israel, there are visits to Arab villages, meetings with people involved with Arab problems, and learning from the environment by preparing questionnaires and summarizing the results. There are also surveys of current events in the Arab world. Every pupil chooses one country and is responsible for gathering information from newspapers and periodicals and making it available to all. Once or twice each trimester, the group meets with Arab lecturers and discusses the material being studied. The topics for term papers include "Oil and the Arab World," "The Suez Canal," "Agrarian Reforms in Egypt," "Agriculture in the Arab Village," etc.

Sample Outline: Course in Underdeveloped Countries

Aims of the course: during the 1950s the process of liberation of colonial countries received a marked impetus. Many states achieved political independence but remained economically backward. Why does political independence not always lead to economic development? What is the main element in economic independence and development?

Participants: 12 students from the eleventh and twelfth grades.

The study was pursued on three levels: individual work and classroom discussions; lectures by the teacher; and theses and library work.

The written work was accompanied by reading material and followed by class discussion. Students read material which presents different aspects, reasons for backwardness, and various solutions. Different political and social views are presented on the same question. Class discussion ensures that the material has been absorbed, and an attempt is made to develop tools of analysis that help in deciding between various outlooks. The methods of study are in line with the general principles of the project method; special emphasis is placed on compositions, lecture preparation, experiments, and model surveys.

In the final year of high school, each student prepares a special thesis;

the subject of his choice is usually connected with his area of specialization. Some sample outlines of theses follow:

Social Factors in Juvenile Delinquency in Israel. Outline: description of delinquency and neglect among youth; origins of delinquency, psychological and social; integration of various groups of immigrants; results of delinquency; remedies for delinquency, past and present. Practical work: visit with a parole officer; visit to a Haifa slum under the direction of the parole officer; visit to a special school for juvenile delinquents and neglected children.

Tolstoy's World Outlook as Expressed in His Work. Morality; faith and religion; social relations; problems of the peasants; agrarian problems; the death motif; general world outlook.

My Environment. The Kinnereth Valley; boundaries of the area; the Kinnereth Valley County Authority, including the City of Tiberias and the northern and eastern shores of Lake Kinnereth. The remains of early agriculture Yarmuk culture; primitive man—the Nachal Amud caves; Tel Abudia and a survey of the Jordan area (Alumot, Ber Zera, Afikim, Ashdot, the slopes, Gesher); origins and history of Tiberias; the Hot Springs of Tiberias in the past and present; natural vegetation of the Jordan Valley: the Gordon House; the National Water Authority and the Kinnereth; social structure of Tiberias—veterans and newcomers, sources of income; agriculture in the Jordan Valley, irrigation projects, cultivated area, crops; kibbutzim in the Kinnereth Valley—structure, economic cooperation, industry, educational institutions; the Kinnereth Valley during the War for Independence.

Our Soil. Analysis of typical farm soils—to a depth of 120 cm.—to determine the agricultural potentiality: mechanical composition of the soil, density, drying point, pH, percentage of organic material.

The Democratic Idea. Formal democracy; the contradiction that democracy creates in a capitalist society; democracy and socialism (democracy in the kibbutz); democracy in Israel; summary.

Other projects for theses are:

The Political Struggle for the Establishment of the State of
    Israel in the International Arena
Life of the Bedouins
The Israeli Folk Song
Realism in Twentieth-Century Literature
The Role of the Village in the Chinese Revolutions
The Kibbutz Movement and the Hagana
Shlonsky's Nature Poetry
The War for Independence in Literature
French Society in the Works of Balzac
Fascism—Its Nature and Manifestation in Various Countries
The Struggle between Materialism and Idealism in Philosophy
The History of Colonial Rule
Anti-Semitism

We have linked the differentiation of courses of study with nonselective education; this is clearly necessary for the individualization of
the learning process and for providing the opportunity to choose fields of
special interest even within our limited framework.

Unity of Education and Instruction

Instruction and education of the total personality must be inseparably
connected; otherwise the educational process is impaired. Outwardly,
there appears to be no disagreement on this basic issue, and modern
educational literature emphasizes the integration of educational activity.
It is concerned with encompassing, as far as possible, every aspect of the
child's life, and not merely with the development of intellect.

The reality, however, is quite different. During the past century, the
school has become an institution that imparts knowledge, and the students are objects into which to stuff information. The school has
neglected every aspect of education except scholarship—a neglect that is
even more serious today, when the family structure has undergone so
many basic changes. The educational role of the family is more limited,
but the influence of the street, an environment that is not subject to
educational supervision, has grown.

Though knowledge is extremely vital, it is not the supreme life value. To impart only knowledge, without character training, does not automatically ensure the acquisition of social and ethical values, without which there can be no real education. Recent studies concerning the attitudes of youth to national and racial prejudices undoubtedly prove that knowledge alone has no beneficial influence on racial and nationalistic prejudices. It is no wonder that good educators throughout the world are concerned with the educational bankruptcy of the school and are seeking ways to ensure *integral education.*

True, there is danger that the teacher, even in the kibbutz, will minimize his interest in the various aspects of the child's life and limit himself to academic achievements and intellectual development. But there is no doubt that every kibbutz teacher must feel the responsibility for total education, even though he may not always succeed in practice.

The integral approach to education and instruction finds its expression in the role assigned to the pupil in the educational process. Good education ensures learning achievement—just as good instruction enhances education—in the broader sense. We well know that disturbances in one area of the child's life leave their mark on other areas, and it is difficult to isolate them. Learning difficulties are not always due to lack of ability or to laziness—they may stem from illness, a particular mental state, conflicts with parents, etc. It would be useless to try to improve learning achievements if we do not understand the reasons for the failure.

On the other hand, we know that good teaching, interesting and significant organization of the subject matter, stimulation of the child's natural curiosity, relevant connections between the learning situation and the everyday environment, independent activity and discovery—all these ensure maximum success and a concomitant satisfaction from the subject matter, increase the child's sense of security, and assure him future success in studies as well as in other areas of life. Consequently, his whole personality is strengthened.

The Peer-Group Unit

The group as a central factor in adolescent education, its importance in the life of the young and its problems, is discussed in detail elsewhere. Therefore, a few remarks about the place of the group in the learning process will suffice.

We will treat the important question of evaluation, marks, and examinations in detail later. However, in this connection, we should mention that if we are successful in maintaining discipline without grades and final examinations, much of the credit is due to the role of the group, which is directed by the educator. Encompassing the totality of its members' lives, the group sees its main function as concern with group learning as well as with the achievements of each individual. The group committee, and sometimes the entire group, discuss day-to-day learning problems, review study plans, discipline members who are not advancing as they should, etc.

Education for Work

Let us deal with this subject only as it relates to the learning process, since it is discussed at length elsewhere. Besides being an important factor in collective and social education, work provides numerous possibilities for variety and enrichment in the learning process. Permanent and systematic contact with the agricultural branches and with production processes, as well as with the technological-scientific developments that are omnipresent in the kibbutz, is a never-ending source of intellectual motivation to acquire knowledge, both formally and in direct contact with the surrounding reality. Two key practices are aimed at enhancing the learning value of work and minimizing the danger of boredom and monotony: (1) until the last year of schooling, each student changes his work place three times a year, and (2) he works with animals, in the fields, and in one of the services each year.

Of even greater importance is the existence of the *school farm, where the younger children, in particular, work,* and where the older children serve as guides and organizers. Adult agricultural advisers impart knowledge connected with the work and adapt it to the various age groups. The children's feeling of responsibility for their farm and for the variety of branches and work processes makes the farm a genuine factor in learning. Tenth and eleventh graders attend agricultural study circles to familiarize themselves with at least two or three farm branches. Emphasis is placed on touring the farm and following developments in one branch during the entire year's cycle.

It would be wrong, however, not to mention the limitations on the students' work. In the higher grades, they work two or two and a half hours every day, and the work is not always easy. Under other conditions, this time would undoubtedly be devoted to studies and homework.

Cooperation Between Teachers and Students.
Directed Independence

On the question of the educator's role and his relations with his students, there were many distortions in progressive education, and some of these misunderstandings once penetrated the kibbutz movement. We refer to the naive conception that the spiritual forces within the young person will grow and develop independently and spontaneously if we refrain from interference and guidance. According to this point of view, the good educator stands aside, prevents danger, and attempts to create optimal conditions for self-development.

In Kibbutz Artzi, under the influence of the youth movement, we saw the adult educator as the center of educational activity and the major precondition for its success and effectiveness. We were never under the quasi-progressive illusion of seeing the educational process as automatic and independent, deriving its strength from "within the child." The spiritual, cultural, and moral values which education must impart to the younger generation are not biological values; they are social values, and do not exist outside of society and its influence. These values must be learned and acquired spontaneously or in an organized fashion, for they are not rooted in the individual biological development of the child. This is the task of the educator as the representative of adult society—the active role of transfer, guidance, and instruction.

This is the foundation upon which relations between teachers and students should be based in the instructional process, which is only one facet of the total educational process. On the one hand, teachers should not be the main actors; on the other, they should not stand aside. The active participation of students in the learning process requires guidance, discrimination, and supervision, without which there can be no assurance of desirable educational results.

The problem of classroom discipline in the kibbutz school rests on this same foundation. It is impossible to maintain formal authoritarian discipline—even if we wished to, we could not succeed. But this does not mean an avoidance of discipline and authority, for there can be no learning or education without discipline. The question is, rather: What will be the nature of this discipline, and what relations will prevail between teachers and students? Mutual respect, understanding for the young and their problems, active participation in the life of the children and not just in the classroom, individual and group guidance, maximal cooperation in study, planning and supervision these are rock-bottom foundations.

Psychological-Educational Principles

Internal motivation versus grades and tests. From the outset, we saw the impossibility of including in our educational system the element of individual competition and its concomitant grading system, both of which contradict a kibbutz social order based on cooperation. Grades have another disadvantage that is no less serious than competition: they are an external motivation that has nothing to do with the learning process itself, such as rewards (good grades), fear of punishment (poor grades), competition with others, seeking the teacher's or parents' approval, etc.

As opposed to all these methods, one should stress the importance of the internal motivation which is intrinsic to the learning process itself— e.g., *interest* in the subject matter, satisfaction with success, the desire to complete a job, etc. Internal motivation is more effective, deeper, and leads to better understanding, to the transfer of learning to other areas, and to improved memory. Jerome Bruner, in his well-known book *The Process of Education*, cites "the magic of discovery" and "self-reward through success" as the main motives for good learning.

With the abolition of grades, examinations that determine the student's fate and the continuation of his studies come to an end. Since there is no selection in kibbutz education, there must be individual concern for each student, for his abilities and talents. From this point of view, the traditional system of grades and examinations has no significance; yet the student's achievement must be evaluated, not in order to compare him with others or to draw conclusions about his future but to give him information about his achievements and errors, how he can correct his mistakes, and how he can advance in accordance with his ability and past achievements.

The kibbutz teacher evaluates the progress of his students in two ways: (1) he undertakes personal contact and consistent follow-up of the accomplishments and efforts of every pupil; and (2) the relatively small class of not more than 25 pupils makes it possible to know every student and to follow his participation and progress.

The fact that there are no final examinations or formal grades does not mean that learning is voluntary and depends only on the good will of the child. Learning is a definite social duty, and the child is not permitted to stop learning. Without using force and punishment, we depend on the personal authority of the educator, the social authority of the group, the children's society, and kibbutz public opinion. These are very powerful forces which, if used wisely and properly, will obviate the need for coercion and punishment.

Individualization and collective effort. We have already noted the special importance of individualized attention in kibbutz education. Theoretically, the kibbutz is responsible for the growth and development of each child, without exception, and it must find suitable ways to do so in accordance with individual abilities and interests. This is the socio-logical-collective aspect of individualization.

The necessity for individualization in learning, however, stems also from two vital psychological and educational considerations: (1) Learning is in essence an individual process. The fact that the teacher instructs does not ensure that the child will learn. Teaching means bringing the individual student to the point where he will learn by himself, in one way or another. (2) In the most homogeneous group of children, there are many individual differences. Any method of instruction that assumes that everyone learns the same thing in the same way will fall short of its educational goal.

These two basic facts are not new, of course. But *in practice*, and especially in the last few generations, with the development of mass education, the school has been based on the "average" child and on the assumption that children of the same age will reach similar achievements if they are given the same subject matter in the same way. Adherents of the "progressive" method in the 1920s and 1930s raised the demand for individualized attention, but the results were few and mainly in the primary grades of the elementary school (except for experimental schools like Winnetka and Dalton, which made an important contribution to the development of revolutionary teaching methods based on far-reaching individualization).

Today, the dominant conception is that individual differences are *desirable* because every society needs different kinds of people and different abilities in various areas. Hence, differences should be nurtured, and each individual must be permitted to develop his talents and inclinations to the maximum.

Consideration for the individual has always been a central principle in kibbutz education, and not only in the school setting. Love for the child, respect for his personality, and seeing him as a complete person have always required special consideration for every child. In the learning process, the main tool of individualization is the project method, which affords the teacher the opportunity to adapt the content and level of the material to the particular needs and abilities of each pupil.

Individualization is only one aspect of the learning process. The other complementary aspect expresses itself in the fact that learning, while basically individual, is also a social process. *Classroom discussion and clarification*, under the skillful guidance of the teacher, excite and enrich intellectual activity to a great extent. The acquisition of knowledge and of intellectual ability is only one of the functions of the group which encompasses every aspect of its members' lives. It is impossible to conceive of collective work not playing a central role in the educational process. In fact, the project method promotes class discussion of learning problems and leads to joint summaries of chapters or of an entire project. The very idea of the project organically merges collective work with individual work: everyone is busy with the same central theme for a definite time period, and every individual works according to his pace, ability, and interests, sometimes alone on one phase of the project while his comrades are working on another.

Learning how to study. We are more conscious today than ever before that knowledge acquired in schools, even in schools of higher education, is of little use if it does not enable and encourage the student to learn throughout his life. Robert Oppenheimer once said, "Most of what is known today could not be found in any textbook when we went to school; we couldn't know it if we hadn't learned since then." He also pointed out that the quantity of knowledge doubles every ten years. The fact that what is being learned is becoming antiquated at an ever-increasing rate forces us to learn continuously and underscores one of the main tasks of the modern school: to teach how to study and to impart the desire to continue learning.

In the last analysis, the problem of transfer of learning is simply the problem of learning how to learn additional things—the dialectical evolution of this problem is well known. Until the end of the nineteenth century there was a naive idea that the learning of certain subjects, such as Latin grammar or mathematics, automatically ensured mental development and added to learning ability. Several experiments performed at the beginning of the present century proved the inaccuracy of this conception. The approach that there is no transfer, and that all learning is specific and cannot be applied outside its sphere, was accepted until very recently. This conclusion was all too hasty, and today, after considerable research, the following formulation is accepted: There is transfer of learning, but it is not automatic or unconditional; the most important condition for transfer is good learning, which emphasizes what is significant, is not submerged in unimportant details, and is concerned with the maximum understanding of principles.

This conception, unopposed in modern psychology, formed the

groundwork of our approach to instructional problems even in the early 1930s, when we began our work. We must admit, however, that we were not always certain of its validity. The theory is easy to formulate and logically convincing, but quite difficult to carry out in practice; and even today there is considerable searching, questioning, and difference of opinion regarding methods to ensure its success. How much more difficult it was when we were without experience and had only primitive tools at our disposal! Many teachers lost confidence, and the results were far from brilliant. In many cases, acquisition of knowledge and memorization of facts were stressed at the expense of the main element of good learning: emphasis on principles and imparting the will and ability to continue learning.

In attempting to formulate the psychological and educational principles of our method of instruction, we confidently reemphasize this principle, knowing full well that it is still not easy to carry it out in practice today. The project method, as compared to the prevailing system of separate subjects, undoubtedly provides more opportunities for meaningful teaching, for sustaining the interest of the majority of the pupils, for limiting unimportant details, and for instilling the desire and the skill to continue studying.

Activity and independent study by the pupil. The importance of pupil activity in the teaching process need hardly be stressed. In the final analysis, the best and most efficient teaching is worthless if it does not activate the pupil and bring him to the point where he will learn by himself. Despite this well-known and agreed-upon elementary truth, most teachers deceive themselves again and again with the notion that if they actively and enthusiastically explain and lecture, the pupil will learn. Apparently, as in the case of other nice ideas, it is easier to formulate theories than to carry them out in practice. Habit and the path of least resistance, both of which are powerful factors in education, are the main enemies of all kinds of good ideas. Hence the importance of the *obligatory organizational framework*, which forces the teacher to continuously strive to ensure the activity and independent study of each pupil. The project method is the means to fulfill this very important task. We often hear the complaint that it demands too much of the teacher and makes his job more difficult. On the contrary, that is one of its chief advantages: it forces the teacher to avoid the beaten track and to resist the temptation, characteristic of traditional teaching, to lecture and refer to one text.

Here are two examples:
Botany Workshop (Ninth Grade)
The field study was carried out during the week of April
14-21. Two days were devoted to setting up the camp, and for
the summary and the breaking of camp; six days were spent on
study.

For security reasons, the field study was not carried out
earlier, as had been planned. It was decided to use the campsite
as the summary point for a scouting unit. The youth movement
leader joined the group and some of the evenings were devoted
to discussions.

The camp was set up near the Damon police station, in a
beautiful forest not far from Bet Oren. We took provisions for
the week so as not to be dependent upon our home. Our main
goal was to become acquainted with the trees and shrubbery in
the woods, and we dealt very little with annuals.

We added additional chapters to the botany study: observation of birds and insects; study of the geology of the Carmel.
The group has a hard core of "nature lovers," who drew most of
the class along with them.

The program went as follows:
Shabbat: Setting up camp, opening program in the evening.
Sunday morning: Field trip at Wadi Damon to the Spring;
    acquaintance with the trees. Afternoon: We divided into two
    groups, one for bird-watching and the other to look for in-
    sects and reptiles. Evening: Discussions about Independence
    Day.
Monday: Hike to Haifa, Independence Day parade, return by bus.
Tuesday morning: Short walk, gathering tree branches and
    shrubbery and learning their classification. Afternoons: Divi-
    sion into subgroups, but in opposite order.
Wednesday: All-day trip to Osafia and then to Yagur. Return via
    Wadi Shomria on the western side of the camp.
Thursday: Descent to Damon Spring; swimming; collecting and
    classifying in groups. Afternoon: Classification and recog-
    nition of main families.
Friday: Walk to Wady Latira. In the evening a party, breaking
    camp, summary, and return home.
Visiting ravens, salamanders, and tadpoles attracted the

attention and enthusiasm of all. A giant wreath of most of the
orchids of the Carmel was placed at the foot of the flagpole. But
the date chosen was not quite suitable—we were at least two
weeks late for height-of-blossom time.

The children were absorbed in the work, and many were
willing to sit for hours and classify the specimens. A project like
this, in addition to its social value, has much to offer in terms of
real contact with nature.

*"Shaehav"—Getting to Know Our Neighbors (Eleventh
Grade)*

During the six years of secondary school, four to eight days
are devoted annually to an extended trip to study another social
environment in Israel—immigrant villages, smallholders' settlements, cities, the kibbutzim of other movements, Arab communities.

Members of two groups of eleventh graders visited ten
kibbutzim—four from Kibbutz Meuchad (Ein Harod, Sdeh
Nachum, Gevat, Alonim), five from the Ichud (Ramat Yocha-
nan, Kfar Hamaccabi, Usha, Yifat, Givat Chaim), and one from
the religious federation (Ein Hanatziv). In the course of these
four days, the pupils participated in the same activities as their
hosts of the same age: they studied, worked, and sometimes
participated in the weekly meetings of the kibbutz.

On the eve of their departure for the visit, the students were
given a questionnaire for use as a guide in understanding the
economy, social problems, and issues related to education,
work, cultural activity, and relations between the generations.
They tried to obtain answers to their questions by meeting
members of the secretariat, by discussions with their peers, and
through personal impressions.

At first the children were very hesitant and uncomfortable at
the idea of coming to a strange place and trying to penetrate an
unfamiliar way of life. But they soon established contact with
their own age group in the settlement, and there was a free
exchange of ideas and constant comparison of the problems of
both homes. In many cases, they accompanied their hosts to
their parents' rooms. It was only natural that they should be
especially interested in the problems and life patterns of the
local youth. In addition to differences in teaching methods,
they were particularly impressed by the lack of an active "children's society" like their own. They also noted differences in the

role of the parents' room in setting the tone for group life.

On their return, the students were generally more alert to various aspects in the life of kibbutzim in other movements and were willing to discuss the problems among themselves. Their comparisons did not result in a preference for another form of kibbutz, but it was certainly a stimulating experience *that broadened their horizons. By comparing their impressions, writing a report, and organizing a summary discussion, their ability to objectivize an experience was enhanced.

Cooperation rather than competition. Individual competition, upon which the grading system is based, is alien to the climate of the kibbutz and has no place in its social framework or in its educational system. Organization of the learning processes in our school must be firmly grounded on cooperation among students and not based on competition.

Our opposition to interpersonal competition also stems from more general educational and psychological considerations; these will be briefly mentioned. Recent research to trace the influence of cooperation and competition in the school has shown that while interpersonal competition was a motivating force in certain cases, especially at a young age, in the final analysis the learning was not more efficient. In his *Learning and Human Abilities* (1961), Klausmeier concluded that in none of the studies did competition lead to more efficient learning than did cooperation, since cooperation lessens the threat of failure for the pupils of lower ability. In his opinion, the school must seriously consider limiting the competition among students in the ordinary classroom learning situation.

These studies demonstrate the educational dangers connected with competition even in a social order that nurtures competition, as in the United States of America. Defeating others becomes more important than doing the job itself. Since, in any competition, only a few can win while the majority must lose, one of the most obvious lessons drawn by most students is that they must protect themselves from the fear of failure by a low level of expectation, lower than their actual potential. From the beginning, they strive not to be among the lowest achievers, but they also do not strive to win. Worst of all, competition encourages the harmful approach of "why work if there is no reward for hard work?"

J. L. Cronbach, whose *Educational Psychology* deals with such attitudes, has summarized the problem with an important observation, namely, that competition reflects the school's intention to encourage the most gifted. The school of the twentieth century, however, undertook the responsibility of developing every pupil to the greatest extent possible.

If such a formulation concerns education in a society based upon competition, certainly there is no place for competition in the kibbutz school, where cooperation and mutual aid are fundamental and competition is so alien. The project method in the earlier grades is by its very nature based on maximum and diversified cooperation among students, and is most decisively expressed in the common project carried out every year in each of our secondary schools and involving every class in the the school.

What is a common project? A program of study that unites the efforts and interest of all the students and teachers around one central problem for a period of three to eight days. The common project satisfies the needs of our secondary schools, which seek to be more than conventional schools. It is an attempt to break down the barriers between classes—not merely for holidays, parties, and joint discussions but also in the central activity of learning. The ability to concretize, which is sometimes neglected in everyday learning, comes to the fore in the common project, and art, crafts, music, and foreign languages are also integrated. Last but not least, special learning units handled in unusual ways can expand the interest of teachers and pupils and have an impact on other learning units and projects. An example of the common project follows.

The Federation of Labor and Its Institutions

Facts

Foundations: history of the workers' movement in Israel; founding of the Histadrut; the workers' society.

Organizations: organizational and administrative tools; conventions and council meetings; statistics.

General frameworks: the trade union; Federation of Agricultural Workers; Council of Women Workers; Organization of Working Youth.

The independent workers' economy: agricultural settlements; cooperatives; industrial and building projects; marketing institutions; financial institutions.

Mutual aid and social insurance: "Kupat Cholim"—health insurance; "Mishan"—aid to the needy; "Dor l'dor"—old-age pensions; pension and mutual benefit funds.

Cultural and educational projects: the cultural and educational center; "Hapoel"—sports; reading rooms and archives; educational centers.

Publications: *Am Oved* (issued by Workers' Publishing House); *Davar,* a daily newspaper; publishing offices of the kibbutz movements; publication of Workers' Councils.

Well-known personalities in the Histadrut.

Problems: parties in the Histadrut; the Histadrut and the State of Israel; private capital and the Histadrut.

Trends: opportunities for development in the future.

Methods of working out the project. As far as content is concerned, the common project is based upon the assumptions that only a few sections are learned by all the groups and that most of the material is divided, according to difficulty, among the groups. Even within the group the material is subdivided into smaller work units. Summaries of the chapters are presented to all pupils in various ways. The methods of learning are the usual ones: reading and independent study, class discussion, written summaries, lectures by students and teachers, quizzes, etc. After a teachers' committee has adapted the material, supervision of the proper conduct of the project is assigned to a joint committee of teachers and pupils.

Division of material according to age level.

All ages: founding of the Histadrut as reflected in statistics; important institutions; literary sections describing the life of workers in the city and in the village; the workers' struggle against natural difficulties and their efforts to improve economic and social conditions.

Seventh and eighth grades: personalities in the Hebrew workers' movements; role of the Histadrut in building the country; members of the Histadrut in the Hagana [self-defense units] and in the organization of illegal immigration; industrial and building projects; marketing institutions (Tnuva, Hamashbir, etc.).

Ninth and tenth grades: outline history of the workers' movement in Israel; organizational tools; agricultural settlements; the cooperatives; working youth; cultural activity.

Eleventh and twelfth grades: trade unions; financial instruments; ideological trends in the Histadrut; inclusion of the Arab worker in the Histadrut; activity outside of Israel; mutual aid institutions; trends of development in the future.

Additional activities

Within the school:
1. Daily news bulletin summarizing the material learned in each class, descriptive pieces, stories, poems, puzzles, etc.
2. Lectures by local teachers or guests to all classes, or to groups close in age, about central problems.
3. Discussions within the above-mentioned frameworks.
4. Evening programs devoted to poetry and music on "Labor."
5. Films and filmstrips about Histadrut institutions and about building the country.
6. Appropriate decorations of classrooms and public places.

Outside the school:
1. Visit to the Histadrut offices and contact with their administrative personnel.
2. Visit to an industrial enterprise.
3. Meetings with key personalities.
4. Meetings with workers at their places of work.

Concluding activities:
1. Display of pamphlet summaries, compositions, drawings, crafts, charts and graphs, texts.
2. Evening festivity to mark project's conclusion.

Didactic Principles of the Project Method

The principles we have listed are an integral part of the project method, but they can be treated individually. It is possible for other methods of instruction to adopt these same principles, but we think that only the project method is so naturally suited to combine them organically and to create learning situations that facilitate (and sometimes even demand) their practice.

The principles that are unique to the project method, and are not found in any other method, are as follows:

Integration and combination of related scientific disciplines. Despite all the changes made in the project method over the years, it has remained an integrative method that is not bound by the strict tradition of separate and unconnected scientific disciplines. On the contrary, it builds interdisciplinary ties between naturally related subjects.

Modern theory of instruction, to the extent that it is possible to speak of such a theory, tends to emphasize the internal structure of each subject, stressing the separate teaching of subjects. But this is only part of the truth. Parallel with attempts to structure the various subjects, modern education stresses the importance of at least a partial integration of different sciences in order to genuinely reflect the reality outside of the school, in nature, in society, and in scientific developments.

Marshall McLuhan, in his *Understanding Media*, pointed out that the conventional division of the curriculum into subjects is already as outdated as the medieval trivium and quadrivium were after the Renaissance. Since any subject studied in depth necessarily relates to other subjects, McLuhan predicted that if school curricula continue their present patterns of fragmentation, they will ensure a citizenry unable to understand the cybernated world in which they live.

If this is true in the natural sciences, it is certainly true of the social and human sciences, where interdisciplinary connections in reality are even more marked. Any serious educational attempt to impart to children and adolescents an approach to the actual problems of life cannot be tied in with accepted "disciplines" and must base itself, in one way or another, on projects taken from real life and linking several subjects in a natural sequence. It is difficult to see the educational purpose in teaching history, geography, political science, economics, and sociology as unrelated subjects, especially if our aim is more than memorization of specific unrelated facts without any organic connection with reality.

The combining of subjects in one project must be organic, reflecting their actual relations in nature and in society. There should also be differentiation according to age: for younger students, the project should approximate as much as possible the physical and mental world of the child, while in other grades it should link the scientific disciplines and the objective reality of nature and human society. On this basis, we arrive at the second principle.

Retaining the internal scientific structure of the subjects. The need to stress the internal structure of each subject—as a means to impart basic principles rather than isolated details, and to aid understanding and recall of the material—has been emphasized a great deal recently, for example by Jerome Bruner, in *Process of Education*. Indeed, this is a very fruitful idea for teaching theory, although there is some doubt at the moment concerning its application in practice, especially in the social sciences and in literature. In recognizing the importance of the internal structure of the subjects, one might justly ask whether the project method, by its very nature, does not contradict the retention of internal structure.

This question arose many years ago, when the project method in Kibbutz Artzi was in its initial stages. Even before the concept of structure of knowledge was advanced, we discussed the negative effect of the project method on teaching the laws of science and the continuity of each science. It should be pointed out that even at that time, in combining disciplines, we were concerned with retaining the internal laws of each science. In Bertha Chazan's article, "From Generation to Generation," we read:

> Every scientific subject develops a method of thought and ways of analyzing and combining facts which are unique to it and to the subjects closely related to it. Only continuous and extended contact with certain subjects enables one to acquire factual knowledge, to penetrate the internal nature of the subject, and to understand the system of thought upon which it is based. . . . In our opinion there is no contradiction between the project method and these vital needs of learning. On the contrary. . . according to the usual method. . . the factual material of the various subjects is assembled in separate piles with no apparent connection between them. After every lesson, the cord is cut, only to begin again after a day or two; and the next lesson, too, is suddenly terminated by the bell.

A flexible time schedule. One of the technical disadvantages characteristic of the ordinary school is the mechanical division of the school day into equal units, separated from each other by the ringing of a bell. Every time unit is devoted to a single subject, and there is no connection with the previous one. The system leads to dividing the child's school day into six or seven entirely different "subjects"; the child passes mechanically from one subject to another at set time intervals. Since the number of subjects to be acquired become more numerous as human knowledge increases, most of them are studied only two or three times per week. A long time elapses between one lesson and the next, and the child's interest is divided and dispersed among many subjects.

The project method strives for *maximum concentration* of the pupil's interest and effort by combining several subjects and treating no more than two projects simultaneously. Until the seventh grade, the child learns one project at a time, and only a few specific subjects are studied outside the project framework—gymnastics, a foreign language, musical education, etc. From the seventh grade on, pupils study two parallel projects—one in the humanities and one in the natural sciences—as well as a foreign language and the arts. Eight to 12 hours per week are devoted to each project to ensure the necessary concentration and continuity so vital to the learning process.

There is growing evidence in the present-day pedagogical literature about the necessity of dispensing with a rigid schedule and substituting more flexible learning patterns that accord with the differences among various subjects and with the psychology of learning. In practice this is no simple matter, for even the project method requires the formal subdividing of the school day into distinct periods. But by limiting the number of subjects taught simultaneously, as with the project method, two adjacent time units for each project become possible. In that way we develop optimal conditions for cooperative learning, class discussions, individual written work, laboratory assignments, and similar methods that activate the pupil and focus his interest.

The project method has come a long way since the first schools of Kibbutz Artzi adopted it. There have been modifications, especially in its application to adolescents and the secondary school. But its present status cannot be considered final. Every method of education and instruction, however revolutionary and progressive, must be dynamic and sensitive to change or else it is doomed to stagnation. Changes in objective conditions, accelerated scientific advances, and developments in the psychological and educational sciences demand constant reexamination of curricula and teaching methods. In addition, achievements and results must be retested in the light of our goals.

For all these reasons, our system of instruction will face serious tests in the coming years. As we continue to develop our system and render it more effective, remaining faithful to its basic principles, we must be open-minded enough to introduce the innovations demanded by objective scientific changes.

the clinic provides individual treatment for children and their parents

Special Education and Child Guidance Clinic

by Rachel Manor

At one time we had illusions that our educational system might prevent emotional disturbances and that we would not need special services for our children. However, we have discovered that although kibbutz life and education contain some preventive elements, they do not prevent emotional disturbance—in fact, they may even be at the root of some problems. It was in response to such needs that in 1950 we began to create a new profession among kibbutz educators—the "special educator." And in 1955 we established the Child Guidance Clinic of the kibbutz movement at Oranim, on the campus of, and in cooperation with, the Kibbutz Teacher Training College.

Special education includes concern for the education of every exceptional child: children with such handicaps as hard-of-hearing and deafness, severe nearsightedness or blindness, speech difficulties; children recovering from polio; brain damage, cerebral palsy, cardiac weaknesses, or any other organic defect requiring special care. Also included are

161

children suffering from emotional disturbances (psychoses, behavior problems, neuroses). In addition, since both the exceptional child and his family are affected by his special needs, consideration must be given to the role of his parents, his educators, and his educational group.

Without the help of the many doctors and specialists who treat such cases, it would be virtually impossible to rehabilitate handicapped children. However, each expert deals with his own specialty and generally does not see the child as an integral personality in the total setting of his interpersonal relationships. This all-embracing view is essential, for it is not unusual for a child with an organic handicap to develop an emotional disturbance, particularly if his educational environment does not know how to accept a handicapped child and fails to support and assist the family, which is also experiencing difficulties.

In a nonkibbutz family it is sometimes realized too late that the child is handicapped, particularly a first child, because there is no other child against whom to compare his development. Even when the parents sense that all is not well, they tend to overlook this, to delude themselves—it is so difficult to face the bitter truth and to turn to an expert for advice. However, to obtain a clear diagnosis that will indicate how the child's educational environment can help, it is advisable that the exceptional characteristics be discerned as early as possible. Collective education gives a more positive guarantee of early diagnosis than any other form of education, since the child grows up in the children's home and is under observation by a trained eye from the first days of his life. Infant nurses, whose approach is more objective and less affective than that of parents, can be helpful to the latter in connection with overcoming their reluctance to consult the experts. They give emotional support to the parents when disappointments, frustrations, and crises occur.

It is difficult for a kibbutz child to be treated outside the kibbutz. The great distance from treatment centers involves much physical effort in traveling, sometimes for a whole day. The child's daily routine is disturbed, the adult accompanying him loses working time, and the number of children who can be helped is reduced to a minimum. In a survey made several years ago we found that while the plans for child therapy and institutional referrals were carried out only in about 40 percent of the cases, 90 percent of the referrals to special educators were actually helped.

The Oranim clinic serves all the kibbutzim and two moshavim, from Chederah to the Upper Galilee, covering about 100 settlements in which 100 special educators work with 1,000 children. They serve as field workers after receiving basic professional training, individual supervision, and in-service training at the clinic. Some years ago a second clinic was opened in Tel Aviv to serve the kibbutzim in the southern part of Israel.

The special educator begins as a lay worker. He is supervised individually, receives in-service training, and after a period of successful experience obtains his basic training at Oranim. Special educators are not substitutes for professional therapists, nor is it their function to correct the work of poor teachers. They do perform the therapeutic work which therapists outside the kibbutz would not be able to do. The basic setup of kibbutz education, where alert educators are part and parcel of the society, offers the possibilities of activating other kibbutz members to cooperate with the special educator in helping the child—a neighbor, an artist, a tractor driver, a carpenter, a nurse, etc. These volunteers join the special educator in a team consisting of the teacher, the metapelet, and the parents. The special educator is the group catalyst, its leader. His educational-therapeutic tools—dynamic understanding of the child's psyche and of his object-relationships—help him to formulate a corrective program for the child. Remedial teaching strengthens the child's functioning; the child's perceptual distortions are analyzed, and there is directive intervention by exercises (color, language, mathematics). In addition to the conventional methods, emphasis is placed on treatment through learning, concept formation, and education. The special educator uses play therapy and creative materials (drawing, clay, dramatic play) as a basis for catharsis. In general he creates an atmosphere of acceptance which, in the course of time, enables the child to face his difficulties and improve his functioning.

In most kibbutzim the special educator also serves on a committee responsible for all problems concerning exceptional children. In this position he is a key person in his kibbutz, and parents and educators consult him about mental health questions. He is also the intermediary between the Oranim Clinic and his own kibbutz.

A child is referred to the special educator after he has been diagnosed in the clinic and a treatment plan has been outlined. Some children are assigned for two to three hours of daily work with the special educators; others get one hour a week. Some special educators do individual work only; others work with groups. In the course of the last several years, experienced special educators have also worked in neighboring kibbutzim.

1. Yehuda is seven years old, very bright and active. His mother has severe asthma, and several times Yehuda has been present when she had an attack. He started day-

dreaming, cannot get out of his bed in the morning, and is depressed. Some weeks ago the special educator started to work with him. His favorite play is shooting with all kinds of guns that are in the room, and to simulate collisions between cars and planes (the car attacks the airplane from behind and the plane has to be repaired in the garage). It is only one month since Yehuda started to visit the special educator, but he has already changed from a withdrawn to an outgoing child. The special educator has continuous contact with Yehuda's parents and educators, and helps them to handle him.

2. Michael is eight years old and of normal intelligence. He cannot read although he is in the third grade. His parents and educators are very concerned and attempt to do everything in order to teach him. They pressure him— directly by trying every possible didactic method, and indirectly by showing their obvious disappointment in him. Finally, he was told that the special educator would teach him. He went reluctantly, but was astonished when she let him play and made no effort to teach him. After several meetings of this kind, at which Michael played and the special educator accepted everything he did, the child asked her why she did not teach him. She asked him if he wanted to be taught. Then he expressed his anger at those "people" who force little children to do whatever they (the adults) want. She reassured him that with her he could do whatever he liked, and that she would teach him only when he asked her to do so. During the following months he tested the "honesty" of this declaration again and again. The special educator had a hard time with him, but even a harder time with his parents and teacher because they could not accept the fact that he played and made no effort to learn. After three months. the reward: he asked the special educator to help him read a story in which he was interested. She started to teach him, and in a short time he learned to read.

3. Margalith, seven years of age, had suffered from polio when she was two, and her left leg did not grow normally. She could neither run nor jump like the other children in her group. She could not reconcile herself to her handi-

cap, nor could her parents. She attacked the children during their games, had temper tantrums when she did not get what she wanted, and dreamed of becoming an acrobat in a circus when she grew up. The special educator helped her to express her aggressiveness and her anxiety, developed her talents in music and handicrafts, and gave guidance to her parents. After two years, Margalith came to terms with her disability. Her plans changed. One day she said, "When I grow up I will be a special educator like you and help other children, because I know how it feels when one needs help." (Since she was one of our first cases—twenty years ago—I can end this account by stating that she *is* today a special educator in her kibbutz.)

4. Dorith is an eight-year-old girl who has an emotionally disturbed mother and a compulsive father. She could not get up in the morning. She was totally absorbed in such autoerotic activities as rocking, sucking, and masturbating. In the first grade, the special educator started to work with her: she arrived early in the morning, helped Dorith get up and dress, took her to her office, and they had breakfast together. Then they played, and gradually the special educator started to teach her. In an amazingly short time Dorith changed: she became an integral part of her group and started to play with the other children. Only on those days when the special educator had to leave the kibbutz did she become the passive and withdrawn child she had been before.

The special educator's own child is in the same children's group. When Dorith saw the special educator in the kibbutz yard or in the children's house after working hours, she embraced her with such intensity that the special educator and her son were taken aback. The special educator began to withdraw, and Dorith's symptoms returned. The special educator brought the case to her supervisor. She felt that she would find some way of giving Dorith the affection and time needed, but could do so only in her office, where there would be no conflict in her relations with her son or with Dorith. This new arrangement had a good effect on Dorith and she is again functioning better.

This last case demonstrates one of the many problems connected with special education in the kibbutz. The special educator herself is a member of the kibbutz, she has daily contact with the children's parents, and in many cases she has had past experiences with them—positive and negative—in different roles. For this reason, we have developed a method of treatment by the special educator, based on learning theory and on concept formation rather than on the dynamic approach of psychoanalysis. This includes an approach to the healthy aspects of the child's personality, his abilities and strength, rather than to his pathological weaknesses. By expanding and deepening his perception through the creative elements of drawing and sculpturing, we strengthen the child, make him more flexible, and free him from some of the fixations and distortions in his development. He learns new ways of looking at himself and at his environment. We have found firm and lasting changes in behavior and learning performance after such treatment. The method is especially appropriate for the seven- to twelve-year-olds who constitute the majority of our clientele.

This brings us to the clinic and its services. It is no coincidence that the clinic is affiliated with the Kibbutz Teacher Training College, where all the educators of our movement receive their training and where the Institute for Research of Kibbutz Education is situated.

The composition of the 27-member staff (two psychiatrists, five psychologists, plus social workers and psychotherapists)—half of whom are kibbutz members and the other half professional people with a special interest in working with a kibbutz clinic—ensures appropriate professional standards as well as proximity to the realities of our society. Most of the kibbutz members on the staff started as educators (metaplot, special educators, kindergarten teachers, or schoolteachers). They have a great deal of practical experience, as well as years of specialization as psychologists or social workers. In addition to their work at the clinic, most of them are also active in the central educational committee of their own kibbutz, thereby maintaining daily contact with developments "in the field." Some of them are on the college faculty. All these factors underscore the special features of the clinic: a balance between the preservation of a high professional standard through professional contacts and the development of a team approach between the psychological-clinical view and the educational operation. The clinic is also a training center in field-work placement for students at the School for Social Work of Haifa University. Israel has other child-guidance clinics, but a key feature of our clinic is the great importance its staff attaches to education and to close contacts with kibbutz society.

The clinic's procedures include a thorough intake process after each referral, a diagnosis, and a treatment plan (at the clinic or in the kibbutz). The clinic provides individual and group treatment for children and their parents. In the course of one year (September 1968-September 1969) 7,170 hours were spent in clinical work, in addition to 334 hours in psychological and psychiatric examinations. The breakdown of the former is as follows:

Guidance to parents, educators, special educators	60%
Staff visits to kibbutzim	19%
Staff teaching of educators at the Oranim college	17%
Direct child therapy	4%

The children referred to the clinic fall into the following age groups:

0-6.6 years	22%
6.6-12.6 years	55%
12.6-18.0 years	23%

The monthly visit by a staff member to the kibbutz provides the opportunity for screening, working with teams, or guidance to parents and educators.

We regard our work with educators as preventive work. The prevention of mental disorder is of far greater importance and effectiveness than the best possible treatment. If educators know how to observe the children with whom they work, and if they acquire a thorough knowledge of the various developmental stages of children and of the needs emanating from each phase, they are better able to create an educationally healthy climate. Also, their self-awareness is helpful in examining and criticizing their own relationships with the children. If they understand the peer group as the soil in which the kibbutz child grows, and if they use this as an educational lever and can maintain ongoing relations with the child's parents, then we have established the foundation for *primary prevention*. Those on the clinic staff who teach the two-year course for special educators at the college combine their teaching program with group work. They help the educator to gain a comprehensive understanding of his environment, and to form effective relationships with his charges, with other educators in his kibbutz, and with the children's parents. The clinic also trains its students in *secondary prevention*, i.e., they teach an awareness of the initial symptoms that point to mental disturbance in a child; this is done on the assumption, confirmed by experience in clinical work, that the earlier a disturbance is detected, the more effective the help will be.

We have no reliable comparative data at our disposal, but it seems to me that our clinic is exceptional in that, through its field workers (educators, special educators, workers in the central education departments), it can keep a watchful eye on 100 percent of the child population of the kibbutzim. That is why children are brought to the clinic at a younger age, and with less pronounced symptoms, than is the case at other clinics. Usually, applications are made to clinics because of such symptoms of neglect and delinquency as extreme behavioral disturbances; but it is less usual to bring young children suffering from fears, undue passivity, or exaggerated tidyness. We do not wish to give the impression that we have achieved an absolutely satisfactory level of awareness and alertness among kibbutz parents and educators. However, if we compare the measure of alertness in the kibbutz movement with that in other sectors of our country (in towns and villages, and in different social classes), we may say that the kibbutzim enjoy a higher level of secondary prevention, thanks to the many-faceted programs of our clinic.

One staff member is a specialist in remedial teaching; another devotes herself mainly to children suffering from organic handicaps. Aware of the implications of its work to the community, the clinic strives for continuous feedback, for the application of mental hygiene principles, and for the improvement of interpersonal relations in the kibbutzim. Our basic approach consists in pointing out the existing problems and showing the community ways in which it can help itself.

The clinic staff also serve as the main instructors and supervisors of the two-year basic training course and of the in-service training for special educators once a month. In 1970, the fifth two-year course for special educators enrolled students from the four different kibbutz federations. All in all, more than 100 special educators have taken this basic training, and the course is recognized by the Israeli Ministry of Education.

In addition to the activities outlined, we should note the constant supervisory contact we have with a special day-school for those retarded and exceptional children who cannot profit in the regular kibbutz schools. They attend the day-school in the morning, and then return to their kibbutz groups after lunch. In other clinic programs—investigation and intake, diagnosis, and treatment plans, for example—we do not differ from other clinics except for the fact that in the majority of cases we treat the child in his own environment and involve his parents and educators. We make a special point of working with fathers: they participate in the parents' groups, receive treatment or guidance, and learn to fulfill their function as fathers more successfully. This approach reflects the kibbutz reality, which enables fathers to be present and active in contacts with their children, in contrast to the situation of many nonkibbutz families.

supply future teachers with pedagogical and methodological know-how

Oranim – Pedagogical Center of the Kibbutzim

by Menahem Gerson

Seminar Hakibbutzim—the teacher training college of the kibbutz movement—was founded in Tel Aviv in 1939 as an institute to train educators for our movement. The need for this institution was based on the principle that the role of educator within the kibbutz can be assigned *only to a kibbutz member*. Since the kibbutz does not permit hired labor, it should make no exceptions when it comes to educating the second generation.

From very modest beginnings, the college grew rapidly, and many nonkibbutz students were enrolled: members of pioneer youth movements, applicants from moshavim, and city youngsters.

Today, Seminar Hakibbutzim has three branches: Oranim, a Seminar at Beth Berel, and a Seminar in Tel Aviv. Oranim occupies the central position; it is concerned with all functions related to *specific kibbutz needs*. (Two exceptions are the Institute for Physical Culture, in which many kibbutz members participate, and the Family and Child Guidance

Clinic, both located in the Tel Aviv Seminar.) Since relatively few kibbutz members study at the Tel Aviv and Beth Berel branches, we shall devote our attention in the present description to Oranim.

As of 1970, the three branches of Seminar Hakibbutzim had 1,120 students (not including the pedagogical preparatory classes at the Tel Aviv and Beth Berel campuses). About one-fourth of Israel's teachers receive their training in these branches.

Seminar Hakibbutzim is a cooperative institution of three movements—Kibbutz Artzi, Kibbutz Meuchad, and Ichud. Despite some philosophical differences, there is a pervading atmosphere of mutual respect and friendly relations. Student contact helps to reduce barriers between the movements, and long-lasting friendships (even marriages) develop.

The Structure of Oranim. Its Advantages

Like every teachers college, Oranim offers not only training courses for elementary school and kindergarten teachers, but other courses and projects designed to meet specific kibbutz needs. Among the latter we find two courses for high school teachers (in the natural sciences and humanities), as well as courses for music teachers, teachers of arts and crafts, and English teachers. All courses last two or three years. In addition, shorter programs are offered: a two-year course for workers in special education ("exceptional" children), a preparatory class in Judaism (designed for would-be teachers whose background in Jewish matters is insufficient due to their upbringing abroad), two courses for metaplot (one is a one-year course, and the other is a three-month course), and a one-year refresher course for teachers on sabbatical leave. Extensive instructional services are available: a botanical garden, a zoological corner, a large library, and a pedagogical laboratory. Oranim also includes a youth and child guidance clinic (see the article by Rachel Manor), as well as the Institute for Research in Kibbutz Education.

This broad and varied framework has made Oranim the pedagogical center of the kibbutz movement. One hundred kibbutz members work there in various capacities: as directors and teachers of courses, as workers in the guidance clinic, and in other projects (some are employed part-time). Oranim's structure has important advantages: the student's varied curriculum allows him to follow his invididual interests, and it ensures a high level of instruction whereby, for example, the specialist in charge of the botanical garden also teaches agriculture courses and the guidance center psychologists teach the psychology courses. A fruitful meeting ground is provided for a large group of kibbutz members from all three movements, teachers and students alike.

The pedagogical-scientific level of the Seminar attracts hundreds of people every year, even those who are not kibbutz members (in 1970, Oranim had 650 students, of whom 70 percent were kibbutz members). Except for the army, the kibbutz movement has no other facility where young men and women from moshavim, from new immigrant settlements, and from the city can mingle with kibbutz members. Such encounters permit kibbutz ideas to penetrate outside the kibbutz population, while our principles can come face to face with the predominant atmosphere of Israeli society.

Pedagogical Principles

In all the years of its existence, Seminar Hakibbutzim has held that it is not enough to supply future teachers with pedagogical and methodological know-how. The knowledge and understanding they bring with them from high school must be considerably enriched. After all, in the teaching profession there is always a danger of getting into a "groove," a danger that will stifle genuine interest and curiosity. Proper training can counteract this in two ways: (1) by enlarging the cultural-scientific horizons of the teacher-candidate, so that when he becomes a teacher he will be able to stimulate the interest of his pupils in the study material; and (2) by fostering a deeper understanding of children and a readiness to establish closer personal contact with them.

Oranim attempts to proceed on both paths simultaneously. We try to foster the student-teacher's curiosity and ability to engage in various scientific research with the help of skilled professional staff, and to give him the opportunity of a more profound treatment of one or two subjects, according to his preference. Oranim attempts to base its students' work on *internal motivation*. Relations between staff and students are informal and friendly, as is customary in kibbutz life. There are no grades, and no examinations are used to spur the student on, as in the Israeli city schools. The Seminar teacher's duty is to follow the progress of his students, to evaluate their work on the basis of oral classroom reports, to conduct experiments in the natural sciences, and to engage in instructional discussions with students, separately or in small groups. We have also started to experiment with student *self-evaluation*, so that he can improve his methods of expressing himself. For students who come from city high schools, these innovations are surprising. They are accustomed to authoritative relations between teacher and student, to being questioned by the teacher as a test of knowledge but not in order to elicit opinions and to engage in discussions. Our success in creating a new type of pedagogical atmosphere and in teaching desirable methods is partly due to the fact that Oranim classes combine people of different backgrounds. The kibbutz members are generally older than the city students (the former may be as young as 22, but many are considerably older—even up to 40 years of age). Many are parents, which makes it easier for them to influence the classroom atmosphere. A distinguishing feature of the Seminar is the tendency to increase independent study and decrease the role of the teacher as lecturer.

As in every educational institution, the pedagogical reality of Oranim is not as smooth and unambiguous as the description of its principles would indicate. Students who are training for elementary school work have to be "general" teachers; they must study a multitude of different subjects, which makes it difficult to concentrate on subjects of their own choice. Many people on the Seminar staff—especially those who are simultaneously teaching in an institution of higher learning—are accustomed to teaching only by lectures.

What We Emphasize

Most institutes of higher learning are today troubled or confused about the *social values* that permeate the learning process. The situation at Oranim is quite different because the social values of the kibbutz movement determine the atmosphere and the issues stressed. While pioneering Zionism and socialism are taught as special subjects, they are the basic background in the teaching of many subjects, especially the humanities. These values are conveyed not by indoctrination but through open discussion, in confrontation with other value systems. Thus, the social values of our movement serve as a life-giving antidote to the confusion and nihilism so prevalent today. We teach Judaic subjects (Bible, Talmudic literature, Jewish history, modern literature) with a secular orientation. The values of the Jewish workers' movement, which has for over sixty years been the major builder of our country, are a touchstone of everything we teach. Of course, we do not shut ourselves off from the historical past of our nation. As we mentioned earlier, students who did not receive their early education in Israel and are lacking in background courses are given a year-long course in Hebrew language and the history of Jewish culture. But the past is not studied as a hallowed and binding subject; it serves as the historical backdrop of the present era, whose national and social roles form the core of our Judaic studies.

Stress is also placed on inculcating an attachment, on the part of the students, to nature. The Jewish renaissance in Israel demands that our teachers train the sons of those who have been city dwellers for generations, bringing them closer to a life that is rooted in nature and to an appreciation of their country's past and present (this training is directed more to students coming from the immigrant settlements). The teaching of zoology and botany, as well as an intimate knowledge of the geography and archeology of our country, is based not upon books alone. Hikes, microscope work, and the collection of specimens are some of the ways of studying the natural sciences.

The teaching of psychology and pedagogy at Oranim does not merely stress the acquisition of methodological rules and elementary concepts of general psychology. The counselor-teacher in the kibbutz meets the child not only during teaching periods; they also spend many hours together outside the school setting. It is therefore quite logical that Seminar Hakibbutzim always had a *dynamic* approach to psychology, which is the only way a teacher can learn to understand every aspect of the child's life, as well as himself and his interpersonal relations. The attempt to enable the teacher to see himself as he is, and to train him to express his own personality, is a key focus in our teaching of psychology and education. In this connection, the *arts* are given a prominent position in Oranim, and every teacher tries to find self-expression in one of the arts, which will also enhance his future work with children.

Problems Awaiting Solution

The method of pedagogical work described above requires intensive *personal guidance*. Oranim offers guidance for classes or for groups within classes (if the register is larger than 30). Individual guidance is available in connection with the final thesis, and psychological counseling is available to all students.

Nevertheless, these services are inadequate in the light of the need for intensive personal guidance. The reason is financial. Oranim is recognized by the Ministry of Education and receives the same governmental subsidies as every other college in the country. However, Oranim offers a number of courses that are not recognized by the Ministry. Its more varied programs and highly developed facilities (the botanical garden, the laboratories, the extensive library, etc.) require extra expenditures. And even though the tuition at Seminar Hakibbutzim is higher than at other teachers colleges, its income is still insufficient to permit intensive personal guidance. As the Seminar expands, the kibbutz movements cannot satisfy all the requests for new courses.

Two other problems should be mentioned. The first one relates to *practical work* and *observation* in actual classrooms, both of which are important in teacher training. Oranim is just now finding its way in this area. For many years this aspect was neglected, partly due to pedagogical resentment of the customary method of "trial lessons" (watched over by a host-teacher or a supervisor), and partly because in the desire to provide the student-teacher with up-to-date information in the various sciences, the program of studies became too crowded. The second problem is that Oranim lacks an experimental school where its teachers-in-training could practice. Such a school would have to be a kibbutz school, and we have not yet found a way to work this out. In recent years there have been many more attempts to establish patterns for observation periods, correlated with theoretical-didactic training and personal guidance. However, it is still too early to claim that the desired goals have been achieved.

The number of students from the Oriental Jewish communities is relatively small in Oranim. In general they are not attracted to the kibbutz, and the high tuition fee proves an important stumbling block. Possibly, the level of teaching is also too demanding. The directors of Oranim feel quite troubled by this shortcoming, and are convinced that our educational principles and social viewpoint are of great significance in the absorption of immigration from the Oriental communities. Recent research by Professor Smilansky (1970) has shown that Oriental youngsters who have found their way to the kibbutz have attained intellectual achievements that are incomparably higher than those of their peers outside the kibbutz. We cannot give up on this issue. We practice self-criticism in everything we do, which leads to changes, experimentation, and progress in many areas that were hitherto considered practically insoluble.

Two Important Courses

In the collective education system, children are brought up from infancy in small groups: 1,500 metaplot work with such groups. In the past, we were of the opinion that any woman was capable of doing such work by virtue of her maternal instincts. But a new attitude has been developing. The role of the metapelet is a most responsible one, particularly during the years when the foundation is being laid for character formation and basic social attitudes. Her work demands not only a psychological understanding of the child, but also a high level of social tact and insight. She must achieve the maximum cooperation of the parents, especially of the mothers. While metaplot assigned to older children work in cooperation with kindergarten or elementary school teachers, the metapelet of infants and toddlers is on her own, and her responsibility goes far beyond the physical health of the child.

Based on our experience and on the psychological literature, we have concluded that the metapelet cannot rely upon intuition alone—after all, intuition entails many personal and emotional elements whose educational value may not necessarily be the best. The determination of a rational educational approach, added to the natural affection of the metapelet for the children in her care, is an important potential advantage of collective education. We have therefore had to overcome our past prejudices and insist on suitable *training* for metaplot. This was quite a difficult task because of the large number of metaplot, and also because we were unable to learn other methods of training (the metapelet is unique to the kibbutz).

Today, the need for special training for metaplot has become self-evident, the period of training is constantly becoming longer, and the program is continually expanding—in terms of participants and of specialization and variety of courses. For example, we expect to add a special course for experienced metaplot, who will later be counselors for the younger metaplot.

Oranim must also undertake another vital task: *the training of teachers of adolescents*. This is a sensitive and important age, which involves the conscious and deliberate preparation of children for kibbutz life. Seminar Hakibbutzim came to the conclusion many years ago that the role of the teacher of kibbutz adolescents is essentially different from that of the high school teacher in the city. That is why we established our own three-year courses (differentiated into humanistic studies and natural science studies) instead of sending these future teachers to a university. The Ministry of Education recently recognized this program, to which a fourth year—for further study and specialization at one of the universities—has just been added.

The difference between the role of a kibbutz educator and that of a city teacher arises from two basic facts:

1. Education in the kibbutz is nonselective. Every one of our children

178 Menahem Gerson

attends school until the age of 18. This fact makes it necessary for the educator to form ties with all his students, not only the gifted ones; and he must also become their friendly counselor, not merely their teacher.

2. An educator in the kibbutz cannot content himself merely with supplying pupils with information in various subjects. He must, in addition, fulfill a difficult but vital and sensitive task: he must consciously foster in his pupils a positive adherence to the *values* of the kibbutz.

To ensure desirable teacher-pupil relations, their contact should be intense and involve every aspect of the pupil's life: studies, social life, and work. We believe that the "subject teacher," who teaches only one or two subjects, is not suitable for this purpose. We prefer to train a teacher for humanistic studies or for natural science studies, one who can teach all the subjects in his area—at least until the last two years of high school, which require a higher degree of specialization. The kibbutz teacher cannot obtain this type of training at any of the existing universities; the only suitable framework exists in Oranim. After a number of years of actual teaching practice and after he has accumulated experience in his work, the teacher may go on to a university for advanced professional-scientific specialization.

Needless to say, instruction in our teacher-training program is maintained at a high level. Many of the staff members at Oranim are also on the faculty of one of the universities. Oranim is proud of the fact that even at this higher level, and perhaps because of it, the students do their work based on *inner motivation,* without the incentive of degrees and examinations.

Recently the Board of Directors initiated negotiations with the authorities of one of the universities to establish a close organizational tie with some departments and raise Oranim's academic status.

The Institute of Research on Kibbutz Education

For many years research workers in Israel and abroad have demonstrated a deep interest in collective education, and for a long time it seemed that our main role in this connection was to offer full cooperation to these researchers—for example, A. I. Rabin's *Growing Up in the Kibbutz* (1965), which was considerably aided by our cooperation. At that time we had no trained personnel to carry out research on our own. In addition, we were held back by the prevailing opinion (more common in Israel) that a kibbutz member should not do research into kibbutz matters because he was too involved and identified with the subject of his research. We later came to realize that researchers from abraod were themselves biased and could not operate without prejudices.

In the summer of 1963, at the initiative of Oranim, an international symposium was held, and scientists from the United States and England met with central representatives of collective education in the kibbutz. The detailed reports of their discussions have been published in book form, and offer the most authoritative English-language source on kibbutz education to date: *Children in Collectives*, edited by P. Neubauer.

In the course of this symposium our guest-participants gave us strong encouragement to initiate our own research into collective education. Their argument, which we have since heard many times from foreign researchers, was: "After all, you are so much more aware of all the problems of the kibbutz, more than any person coming from outside. You must, of course, beware of preconceived notions. But this caution holds equally for the research worker coming from abroad."

As a result of these deliberations, Oranim set out to establish the Institute of Research on Kibbutz Education. In addition to engaging in research, it also evaluates, confirms, or rejects research proposals in the area of kibbutz education—those proposed by Israeli or foreign scientists. The Institute has been helped greatly by many people from the United States, and we have formed close personal ties with visitors who come to observe the work of Oranim or to do research here. Some of the Institute research has been published, but as yet only in the Hebrew language. In due time we hope to have large parts of this material appear in English.

In conclusion, we see an institution developing at Oranim with a threefold role: training and education, psychological treatment, and research. This institution carries out the specific tasks delegated by the kibbutz movement; but it is also a progressive and invigorating factor in the field of education in Israel because of the hundreds of Seminar Hakibbutzim graduates who go forth every year to teach throughout the country. The kibbutz is not a utopia enclosed within its own walls. It has taken upon itself public tasks which help to shape the life of Israeli society—in politics, economics, culture, and education.

*a happy balance between the needs, inclinations, and predispositions of
the individuals*

Epilogue

by A. I. Rabin

In the preceding pages, a group of kibbutz educators have unfolded the panorama of an educational system that took many years to develop and is constantly undergoing changes and modifications. Although general philosophical principles, of varying degrees of abstraction, are introduced, the bulk of the presentation is a down-to-earth report on the operational aspects of the system—"how it works." What is described characterizes kibbutz child-rearing and education in the late 1960s and early 1970s—a dynamic system that is responsive to its society which, in turn, follows its own evolutionary path, not altogether unscathed by broader national and international developments.

Several important trends that emerge from the contributions are worthy of special emphasis. First, the considerable stress placed upon the family as an educational factor and as a significant influence in the personality formation of the kibbutz child. Many writers have stressed the changes in family structure, the weakening of its influence, the down-

181

grading of its importance. But educators in this volume underscore the undiminished vitality and potency of the family unit. There is even some evidence regarding the strengthening of the family unit and its significance as an educational factor within contemporary kibbutz society. We also see here a more balanced view of *all* the important educational influences in the life of the child: metapelet, other adults, peers, *and* the biological parents and siblings.

A second important principle underlying the kibbutz educational system is the relative clarity of the social values which the society that nourishes it wishes to perpetuate. "Ours is not a neutral education," states one of the authors. A distinct goal is held up and directs the educational enterprise: the perpetuation, and preparation for the perpetuation, of the "collective-communal" society which the kibbutz represents. There is a realistic appraisal of the aimlessness of much of Western education, its stress on "freedom of the individual" and "self-realization." The appraisal implies a certain equivalence and relativity of values. Kibbutz society has a value system in which it believes and which it imparts to the young in order to assure its very existence.

Third—and this may seem rather paradoxical—is the striving for individual self-realization and freedom within the system. At first blush, such a combination of goals may *appear* paradoxical: on the one hand, we see the unabashed and conscious delineation of educational objectives stemming from general ideological sources, and, on the other, the stress on autonomy, democracy, and voluntarism. The kibbutz system emphasizes progressive education and the project method—forms of freedom for the individual child, but within a general structure and framework. Essentially, without implication of cynicism, the kibbutz educational undertaking can be described as characterized by "guided freedom." It is neither anarchic nor oppressive. There is an attempt to reach a happy balance between the needs, inclinations, and predispositions of the individual and the expectancies and demands of the social system—a difficult balancing act, which the concrete examples offered in this book amply illustrate. There is also an admission of individual competitiveness and personal achievement, as well as concern with self-realization and no submission to a totalitarian, monolithic group.

The economic, social, and psychological successes of the kibbutz movement, successes that are frequently documented (Rabin, 1971), are perhaps due primarily not so much to political ideology as to the relative consistency of values and expectancies which are shared by its numbers and to which the children are exposed. To be sure, there are the dynamisms of change, but not the extremities of transience. The child, via his educational experience, enters this relatively secure world. This can be contrasted with the inconsistencies in more pluralistic and less homogeneous societies and social systems, with the considerable instability and transience that have become so characteristic of them.

It is not the purpose of the present volume to point the way to other societies and educational institutions. The aim is merely to illustrate certain alternatives that "work". The reader may be able to find some elements within the material that can serve as ingredients in the evolution of a new and viable educational philosophy and methodology which are so eagerly sought by many thoughtful people in modern society.

REFERENCES

Bruner, J., *The process of education*. Cambridge: Harvard University Press, 1960.

Cronbach, J.L., *Educational psychology*. New York: Harcourt, Brace & World, 1964.

Dewey, J., *Democracy and education: An introduction to the philosophy of education*. New York: Macmillan, 1964.

Erikson, E.H., *Childhood and society*. New York: W.W. Norton & Co., 1950.

Fromm, E., *Man for himself*. New York: Rinehart & Co., 1947.

Hazan, Bertha, *From generation to generation*. Tel Aviv: Sifriat Poalim, 1947.

Isaacs, Susan, *The nursery years: The mind of the child from birth to six years*. New York: Schocken Books, 1968.

Kilpatrick, W.H., *The project method*. New York: Teachers College, Columbia University, 1929.

Klausmeier, H.J., *Learning and human abilities*. New York: Harper, 1961.

McLuhan, M., *Understanding media*. London, Sphere Books, 1968.

Mead, Margaret, Some theoretical considerations on the problem of mother-child separation. *American Journal of Orthopsychiatry*, 1959, *24*, 471-483.

Neill, A.S., *Summerhill*. London: Golancz, 1967.

Neubauer, P. (ed.), *Children in collectives: Child-rearing aims and practices in the kibbutz*. Springfield, Ill.: Charles C Thomas, 1965.

Parkhurst, Helen, *Education on the Dalton Plan*. New York: E. P. Dutton & Co., Inc., 1922.

Rabin, A.I., *Growing up in the kibbutz*. New York: Springer, 1965.

Rabin, A.I., *Kibbutz studies: A digest of books and articles on the kibbutz by social scientists, educators, and others*. East Lansing, Michigan: Michigan State University Press, 1971.

Rapaport, D., The study of kibbutz education and its bearing on the theory of development. *American Journal of Orthopsychiatry*, 1958, *28*, 587-597.

Shapira, A. (ed.), *The seventh day*. New York: Scribner's, 1970.

Stone, L.J., & Church, J., *Childhood and adolescence: A psychology of the growing person*. New York: Random House, 1957.

Whitehead, A.N., *The aims of education*. New York: Macmillan, 1929.

GLOSSARY

Brit Hatnua Hakibbutzit   Union of Kibbutz Movements.

chaver (pl., **chaverim**)   (literally, comrade)—kibbutz member.

chevra   peer group; social milieu.

dunam   land measure unit, approximately one-fourth of an acre.

Hapoel   workers' sports organization.

Hashomer Hatzair   (literally, young guard)—youth organization which furnishes recruits for the kibbutz movement; affiliated with the Kibbutz Artzi federation.

Histadrut   National Labor Federation of Israel.

Ichud   (literally, union)—one of the federations of kvutzot and kibbutzim affiliated with the moderate "Mapai" Socialist party.

kibbutz (pl., **kibbutzim**)   a communal settlement in Israel (literally, meeting or gathering).

Kibbutz Artzi   largest federation in the kibbutz movement, affiliated with the "Mapam" party.

Kibbutz Dati   federation of religious kibbutzim.

Kibbutz Meuchad   one of the three largest federations of kibbutzim; politically, it stands between the Ichud and Kibbutz Artzi.

kvutza (pl., **kvutzot**)   a term used in two ways: (1) a small kibbutz, especially characteristic of the early period of the kibbutz movement; (2) a group of four to six children living together in the children's house; the size of the group is usually increased after the preschool period.

metapelet (pl., **metaplot**)   (literally, caretaker)—an infant nurse and/or housemother in the children's houses of the collective education system.

mosad chinuchi (sometimes **mosad**)   a high school.

moshav (pl., **moshavim**)   cooperative settlement organized primarily for economic goals related to consumers' and marketing needs.

pe'uton   toddlers' house.

Seminar Hakibbutzim   training college for teachers, metaplot, and other educators, established and run by the kibbutz movement.